MW00358960

MISSOURI Studies Government & Constitution

Missouri

CLOUD PUBLISHING
Phoenix, Arizona

Studies

Darryl Stacy

Donald L. Scruggs, Ph.D.

ABOUT THE AUTHORS

Darryl Stacy, Author

Darryl Stacy had more than 20 years of experience as a social studies teacher, district social studies coordinator, and instructor in government and constitution at the college level. Stacy also taught curriculum specialists, administrators, and teachers in instructional skills using the Hunter model. He worked as a consultant in the areas of instructional skills, outcome-based education, and social studies materials development for a number of school districts around the country.

Donald L. Scruggs, Ph.D., Consulting Author

Donald L. Scruggs, Ph.D. is a retired professor of political science at Stephens College, Columbia, Missouri. American politics, particularly legislative studies, remain his principle teaching and research interest. During his tenure at Stephens College he directed the College's legislative intern program.

ISBN 0-911981-75-6
Printed in the United States of America

Contents

TERMS TO LOOK FOR

- agriculture
- Dissected Till Plains
- cash crops
- Osage Plains
- Ozark Plateau
- Mississippi Alluvial Plain
- precipitation
- prehistoric
- mounds
- Louisiana Purchase
- jumping off place
- boodle
- patronage
- progressive movement
- anti-trust
- sharecroppers
- New Deal
- victory gardens
- census
- urban
- rural
- suburbs
- Bible Belt

1

Missouri: Its Background

Missouri is located in the center of the United States. Its borders touch eight states: Iowa on the north; Illinois, Kentucky, and Tennessee on the east; Arkansas on the south; and Nebraska, Kansas, and Oklahoma on the west. Missouri has many different peoples and lifestyles. The land of Missouri ranges from river bottom to rolling hills, prairies, and rugged mountains. The two longest rivers in the nation are in Missouri; they are the Mississippi and the Missouri. The state also has many clear flowing streams. Much of the state is farmland, producing large amounts of food for the rest of the nation and for export to other countries. Missouri has many small towns and large cities. Both farming and industry are important to our state. Education is important, too. Well-known universities, such as the University of Missouri, Washington University, and St. Louis University, are located here. These schools teach a broad variety of curricula, including law, medicine, and engineering. The University of Missouri–Columbia has the oldest journalism school in the world. The people of Missouri are said to be very independent. This independence is de-monstrated even on the state's license plate, which carries the slogan, "Show Me State"!

GEOGRAPHY

Missouri covers 69,697 square miles. It is 19th in the country in land area. The state is divided into 114 counties and the city-county of St. Louis. St. Louis serves as both city and county, and elects its own county officials. One quarter of the state is covered by forest. This means that there are more than 12 million acres of forest land in Missouri. Almost three out of four acres of land in the state are used for some type of ***agriculture,*** which is farming or raising livestock.

Rivers

Three major rivers flow through Missouri. The Mississippi River flows from north to south. It forms the eastern border of the state. It is also the longest river in the United States. This river has long been used to transport products south to the port at New Orleans, Louisiana.

The Missouri River winds through the northern half of the state. It enters Missouri at the northwestern corner and turns east at Kansas City. This river forms the western boundary for the northern part of the state. The Missouri flows into the Mississippi just north of St. Louis.

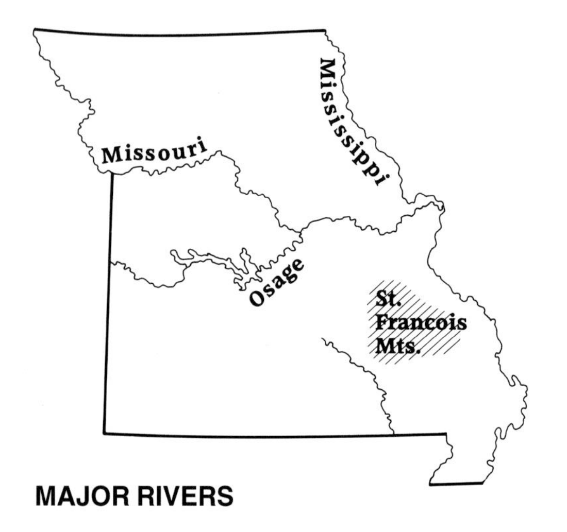

MAJOR RIVERS

The Osage River is located in west-central Missouri. It flows east into the Missouri River. There are also a number of smaller rivers throughout the state.

The Lake of the Ozarks is located on the Osage River. This is the largest lake in the state. It is one of the largest artificial lakes in the world. The lake is created by Bagnell Dam. It has a shoreline of 1,672 miles. It covers about 65,000 acres. There are eight large artificial lakes and many small ones formed by dams in Missouri. Canals and dams have been built on the rivers to help control the effects of drought and floods.

Geographic Regions

The state is divided into four geographic regions. The area north of the Missouri River is called the ***Dissected Till Plains.*** Great ice glaciers once covered this region. Wind brought deposits that made the soil very fertile and well suited for growing ***cash crops***. This area is now covered with farms.

The ***Osage Plains*** are in western Missouri between the Missouri and Osage rivers. This is flat prairie land. The soil is not as rich as the Dissected Till Plains and is used for growing corn and other grains.

The ***Ozark Plateau*** includes most of the southern part of the state. It is located south of the Osage River in the west and south of the Missouri River in the east. This is the largest geographical region in Missouri. It consists mainly of forested hills and low mountains. The plateau rises from 500 feet to 1,700 feet above sea level. The soil is very good for gardening and growing strawberries. There is a type of limestone soil in the southwest part that is good for growing grass and hay. Big Spring is also located in the Plateau. It is the largest spring in the state. About 278 million gallons of water flow from it every day. More than 1,450 caves are found in the state. Many are located in this area. These caves were formed by underground streams. The Ozark Plateau is a popular recreation area and a major tourist attraction.

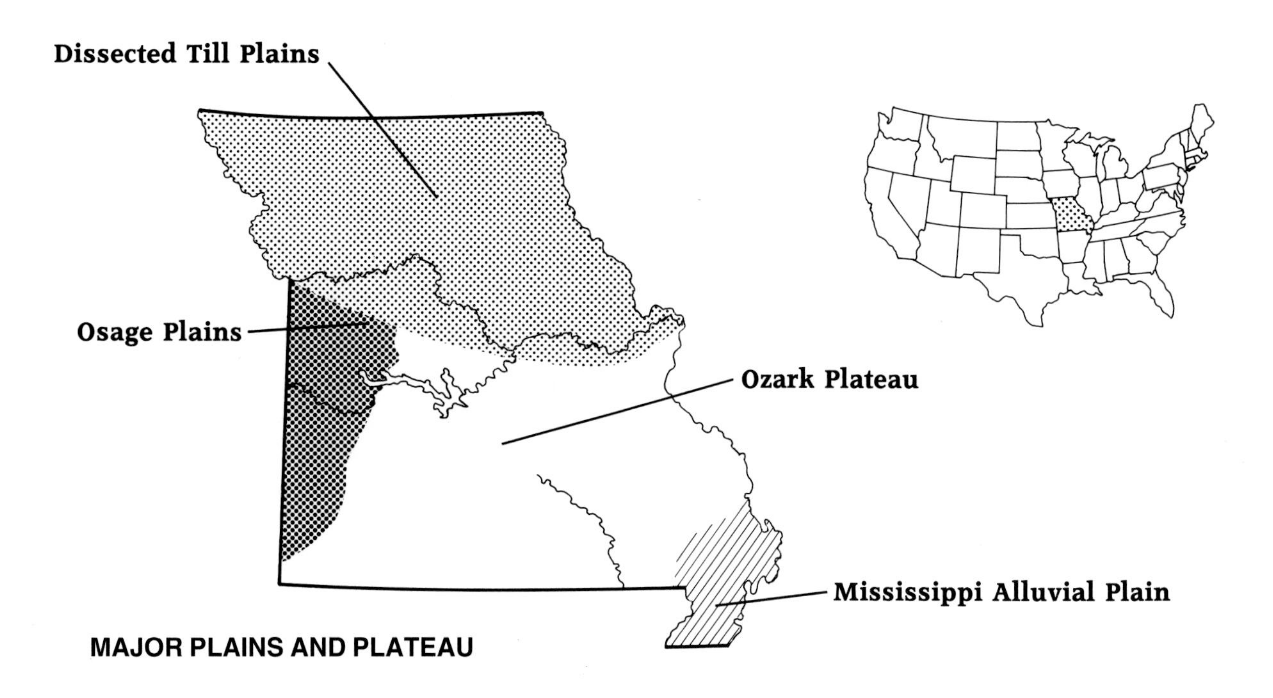

MAJOR PLAINS AND PLATEAU

The fourth geographic area in Missouri is called the ***Mississippi Alluvial Plain.*** It is located in the southeastern corner of the state. This plain is sometimes called the "Boot Hill" of the state. Take a close look at the southeast corner of the state and you can see why. The area was once a swampy wilderness next to the Mississippi River. It has since been drained and cleared, becoming fertile farming land.

Mountains

There are two major mountain areas in Missouri. The Ozark Mountains are located in the Ozark Plateau. They range from 500 feet to 1,700 feet in height, making them more like large hills rather than mountains. There are many large caves and springs in the Ozarks. The St. Francois Mountains are the other mountains. They are located in southeast Missouri, They are not a continuous range, but rather in groups of two or three. One of these mountains has the highest peak in Missouri. It is Taum Sauk Peak and is 1,772 feet above sea level.

Climate

Missouri is far enough south to avoid the severe winters of the northern states. Summers are warm and humid, due to considerable rain.

Both winters and summers are milder in the mountain areas than in the plains. Average summer temperatures range from about 81 degrees fahrenheit (F.) in the southeast, to about 79 degrees F. in the north and in the mountains. The state's record high temperature was 118 degrees F., reached on July 14, 1954, at both Warsaw and Union, and in Clinton in 1936.

Winter temperatures in the state are often below freezing. In January, temperatures vary from 29 degrees F. in the north, to about 38 degrees F. in the southeast. Missouri's record low temperature was -40 degrees F. set at Warsaw in 1905.

Average precipitation each year ranges from about 50 inches in the southeast to 30 inches in the northwest. ***Precipitation*** means rain, melted snow, and other moisture. The climate gives the state a long growing season, from about 225 days in the southeast to 170 days in the north.

Q:

What are the 10 most important geographic features of Missouri?

DISCUSSION: HOW DO THE GEOGRAPHIC FEATURES OF THE STATE AFFECT ITS ECONOMY AND GOVERNMENT?

HISTORICAL BACKGROUND OF MISSOURI

Missouri has a rich history. It was home to mound-building Indians in prehistoric times. ***Prehistoric*** means "before written history." Then came the Osage, Shawnee, Fox, and Delaware tribes.

The area that is now Missouri was included in the Louisiana Purchase. Prior to that, it had belonged to the French and to the Spanish. Missouri became a state in 1821 and was involved in the slavery issue.

Indian Civilization

In prehistoric times, as early as 12,000 B.C., people lived in what is now Missouri. These people left a record of their lives through the things they made. There were several prehistoric civilizations: the Hopewell (500 B.C. to 400 A.D.); the Mississippian (900 A.D. to 1350 A.D.); and the Osage and Missourian (1350 A.D. to 1700 A.D.).

These early people built their settlements close to the rivers in order to grow crops. They built ***mounds*** of earth in which to bury their dead. The Mississippians also built temples on these mounds. They lived in large villages, in houses with square roofs and walls made of rushes and wood. They farmed, fished, and hunted. They were also adept at making pottery and copper jewelry.

Many tribes were living and hunting in Missouri when the first explorers arrived. Some spoke the same language as the Algonquins who lived to the east. Others spoke the language of the Sioux. The Missouri tribe was the strongest tribe living in the area. They lived in large houses with frames made of wood poles. The roofs and sides were covered with reeds. These people hunted and farmed for a living. Another major tribe was the Osage. The Osage also lived in large houses and were farmers and hunters. They hung dried meat, animal skins, and clothing inside their houses.

After the first Europeans explored the area, the settlers began to arrive. They took over the land the Indians had farmed and hunted. As this happened, the Indians began to move west. A peace treaty was signed between the Indians and the U.S. government in 1815. It ended Indian attacks on the settlers. While there are no Indian tribes living in Missouri today, they did leave the state with its name. Missouri is an Indian word that is believed to mean, "the town of big canoes."

Settlement

The first Europeans to come to Missouri were probably French explorers from Canada. Father Jacques Marquette and Louis Joliet wrote the first accounts of exploration in the area in 1673.

The Mississippi valley was claimed for France by Robert Cavalier, whose title was Sieur de la Salle, in 1682. This area included what is now Missouri, though Cavalier called it Louisiana. In 1762 France gave the Louisiana region to Spain, and Spain returned it to France in 1800. In 1803, France sold it

Excavation of land for housing or other large developments is usually done by huge machinery, but for fragile sites like this Indian ruin at Stockton Reservoir at Stockton, the soil is loosened and dug by hand.

to the United States, calling it the *"Louisiana Purchase."*

The French made the first European settlement at Ste. Genevieve in the 1730s. St. Louis was founded as a fur trading post in 1764 by Auguste Chouteau and Pierre Laclede. St. Charles was founded in 1769.

Statehood

Congress made Missouri a territory of the United States in 1812. In 1820, Congress passed the Missouri Compromise. It provided that Maine would become a "free" state and Missouri a "slave" state, meaning that slavery would be allowed in Missouri. The Northwest Ordinance of 1787 had not allowed slavery in the states of Michigan, Illinois, Indiana, and Ohio. The result was that many slave owners moved to Missouri. Many people from the north who opposed slavery also moved to Missouri, creating controversy in the state regarding slavery.

Missourians elected delegates to a state constitutional convention. They completed writing a new constitution in 1820. Congress then admitted Missouri as the 24th state on August 10, 1821. The first state capitol was at St. Charles. Missouri's first governor was a Democrat named Alexander McNair. The state gained another six counties in the northwest as part of the Platte Purchase in 1837.

Missouri Develops

Missouri became the *"jumping off place"* for those who were exploring or moving west. Lewis and Clark began their famous exploration of the west from St. Louis in 1804. Moses Austin and his son Stephen traveled west from Missouri to what was then part of Mexico. They set up a new settlement there that later became the state of Texas. The Santa Fe Trail westward began in Independence. Many people who were part of the great "land rush" in Oklahoma started from Missouri.

The Missouri River attracted farmers to the state. Many settled near major streams. Businessmen built mills there for grinding grain. Cheap land, a team of horses, a cultivator, and hard work were all that were needed to start farming. Many kinds of crops were grown in the state: wheat, corn, hay, tobacco, apples, grapes, nuts, potatoes, and vegetables. Cattle also became a big industry. The state is still a major producer of cheddar cheese and milk. The mule became the trademark of Missouri agriculture. Mules were recognized for their sure-footedness and endurance.

Many famous people were part of Missouri's early history. Some of them were:

- Daniel Boone: explorer and frontiersman
- Manuel Lisa and William Ashley: fur traders
- Joseph Smith: organizer of the Mormon church who settled in Independence in the 1830s
- Kit Carson: frontier scout and trail blazer
- Father Pierre Jean DeSmet: Catholic missionary to the Indians
- Samuel Clemens: author from Hannibal who wrote classic American literature under the name of Mark Twain

The Civil War

In 1854, battles began to break out between anti-slavery forces in Kansas and pro-slavery forces in Missouri. Governor Claiborne Jackson was strongly pro-south when the war broke out. He and most of the legislature moved to southern Missouri af-

Samuel Langhorne Clemens' early career experiences as a Mississippi River steamboat pilot and a reporter, plus his love of travel, gave him the material he needed for his many writings, which he penned under the name of Mark Twain.

ter the war started. There they passed an ordinance to secede from the union. Many Missourians did not agree with this action so they set up another government in Jefferson City that was accepted as the real government by them and the federal government in Washington, D.C., Missouri became a battleground during the Civil War from 1861 to 1865. About 11 per cent of the battles in the Civil War were fought in Missouri. Among these were battles at Carthage, Lexington, and Boonville.

The Late 1800s

St. Louis became the main center of industry in the state after the Civil War. Key industries were leather products, chemicals, lead and iron products, beer, and streetcars. Meat packing and flour milling developed in Kansas City. St. Joseph was another center for meat packing. Two very different industries grew in Washington, Missouri: the manufacture of zithers (musical instruments), and corn cob pipes called meerschaums. Lead mining and the making of bricks and railroad ties were other big industries in the state.

The 20th Century

Many important things have happened in Missouri during the 20th century. In 1904, the Louisiana Purchase Centennial Exposition was held in St. Louis. This brought people to Missouri from all over the nation. It was like a giant fair.

Missouri was known for political corruption in the early 1900s. Members of the legislature sold their votes and influence. Making money this way was called ***"boodle."*** Corruption brought a demand for reform, which helped the Republican party gain some power.

The Pendergast family gained power in Kansas City during the 1920s and 1930s. Tom Pendergast, city councilman, became known as "Boss" because his faction of the Democratic Party gained control of the council and used ***patronage*** to control city hall. Patronage refers to the practice of using relatives and friends in city-paid jobs.

During this period, the ***progressive movement*** gained power. The Progressives wanted to directly elect United States Senators, give women the right to vote, and to make the sale of liquor illegal.

The Louisiana Purchase Centennial Exposition of 1904 celebrated "the greatest bargain in American history"—when the western half of the Mississippi River basin, known as Louisiana, was purchased from France a century before.

Also, ***anti-trust*** lawsuits were brought against big companies like Standard Oil. The purpose of these lawsuits was to break up the big companies so that they would have less power. New election boards were set up and a commission was created to regulate utilities. Utility companies provide electric, water, and gas services.

In 1929, the Great Depression began. It not only hurt Missouri economically, it hurt the entire country. Many people had no jobs; many banks and businesses closed. Unemployed men and boys formed the "Starvation Army" and rode in railroad boxcars from town to town looking for jobs. Many ***sharecroppers*** went broke and had to leave the farms on which they worked. Sharecroppers were small farmers who paid rent on land by giving part of their crop to the owner of the land.

New Deal laws under President Franklin D. Roosevelt brought many government projects to Missouri. The Public Works Administration (PWA) built streets and highways, sewer systems, buildings, and an auditorium in St. Louis. The Works Project Administration (WPA) built parks, pools, airports, and libraries. The Civilian Conservation Corps (CCC) developed many more parks.

The national economy became much better during World War II. In Missouri, all types of ammunition, steel helmets, and explosives were produced. Many people grew ***victory gardens*** of vegetables. More than 450,000 men and women from Missouri served in the armed forces during this war. Two generals, Omar Nelson Bradley and James Harold Doolittle, came from our state.

Harry S Truman, of Independence, was elected Vice President of the United States in 1944. When President Franklin Delano Roosevelt died in 1945, Truman became President. In 1948, he was elected to that office through the vote of the people. A library has been built in Independence to store the records of his administration.

In the 1960s, the Pea Ridge iron mine opened. Spacecraft for the Mercury and Gemini programs were produced by the Boeing aircraft company. This company has a large plant in St. Louis. Aircraft and space technology have become a big industry in the state today.

In 1965, the Gateway Arch in St. Louis was completed. It is meant to be a symbol of the gateway to the west. It is the nation's tallest monument, standing 630 feet high.

Also in 1965, the civil rights movement came to Missouri. A law was passed to make racial discrimination illegal in public places.

Q:

WHAT CHARACTERISTICS OF MISSOURI TODAY CAN BE TRACED BACK TO EVENTS IN ITS HISTORY?

Harry S Truman also helped to name Missouri's state song. When he became President in 1945, he loved listening to "The Missouri Waltz." It became the official state song four years later.

The Gateway Arch in St. Louis sits on 91 acres of St. Louis' old commercial district where pioneers outfitted themselves for their westward journey across prairies, mountains, and deserts.

Today you can take a four-minute tram ride to the top of the arch where you can see barges pushing loads of corn and coal down the Mississippi River.

DISCUSSION: What was the importance of Missouri to the development of the nation?

PEOPLE

The 2000 ***census*** showed a population of 5,595,211 in Missouri. Missouri is now th 17th largest state in the nation. The number of people in the state has not grown at the same rate as the nation since 1900. About two-thirds of Missouri's people live in urban areas. ***Urban*** areas are cities or towns of 2,500 people or more, according to the census bureau. Cities have an organized local government, while towns may or may not be governmentally organized. Those without, for example a rural subdivision, look to county government for services.

The other one-third live in the remaining ***rural*** areas. Some cities have shrunk in population since 1970. Most of the suburbs have grown but some older ones have lost population, similar to the central cities of Kansas City and St. Louis.

Suburbs are newer cities and towns that have developed on the borders of older central cities. Many people live in suburbs but work elsewhere.

St. Louis is the state's largest metropolitan area. It is located on the eastern border and had 1,364,504 people in 2000. The second largest metropolitan area is Kansas City, located on the western border. Both areas have many suburbs, but the St. Louis metropolitan area has the most. St. Louis County has 91 county communities in 2003. Examples are Florissant and University City adjoining St. Louis City, and Lee's Summit and Gladstone bordering Kansas City.

Gladstone is surrounded by Kansas City through the ability of Kansas City to easily annex territory. However, the state law was changed by the

General Assembly in 1976 to make it more difficult for cities to annex, therefore fewer city-initiated annexations have occurred.

Only two percent of the people in the state were born in another country. More than half were born in Missouri. Eighty-nine percent of the people are called caucasian. People of African-American ancestry form about ten percent of the state's population. They live mainly in St. Louis, Kansas City, and the southeast corner of the state. The last one percent of the people represent other ethnic groups.

The state is considered to be part of the ***"Bible Belt."*** This means that many people are Protestant fundamentalists in religion. One out of six Missourians is Catholic. They live mostly in the urban areas.

The people are employed in many kinds of jobs. The main sources for jobs are manufacturing, agriculture, tourism, mining, and transportation. The average income for families in Missouri is a little below the national average.

Q:

WHAT ADJECTIVES WOULD YOU USE TO DESCRIBE MISSOURI'S PEOPLE?

RESEARCH: FIND OUT ABOUT THE PEOPLE WHO LIVE IN ANOTHER STATE FROM WHICH YOU OR SOMEONE IN YOUR FAMILY CAME. HOW ARE THE PEOPLE IN THAT STATE DIFFERENT FROM THOSE IN MISSOURI? HOW ARE THEY SIMILAR?

Children standing outside of the Mark Twain Home and Museum in Hannibal, Missouri, depict characters from Twain's popular stories for and about children, "The Adventures of Tom Sawyer" and "The Adventures of Huckleberry Finn."

❒ SUMMARY

Missouri is a very diverse state located in the heart of the nation. It is the 19th largest state in land area, which has been divided into 114 counties and the city-county of St. Louis. Three major rivers flow through the state: the Mississippi, the Missouri, and the Osage. The largest lake is called Lake of the Ozarks; it is a man-made lake created by Bagnell Dam that provides recreation as well as flood control.

Our state is divided into four major geographic regions: The Dissected Till Plains, the Osage Plains, the Ozark Plateau, and the Mississippi Alluvial Plain. The Ozark Mountains are located in the Ozark Plateau. The St. Francois Mountains are located in southeast Missouri. The state has a moderate climate with a long growing season. Summers are humid due to frequent summer rains.

Missouri has had a colorful history. The area was settled by Indians as early as 12,000 B.C. These prehistoric people hunted, farmed, and built mounds in which to bury their dead. Later tribes built large houses. The Indians moved west as settlers moved into this area. The French were the first to explore and settle Missouri. It was part of the large area then known as Louisiana. Both Spain and France once owned it, but France sold it to the United States in 1803.

Statehood was granted to Missouri in 1821. The many rivers and good climate attracted farmers and settlers. Soon Missouri became the "jumping off place" for those who were going farther west. Because of our excellent soil, businesses that were based on farming grew quickly. Since Missouri was admitted to the Union as a slave state, it soon became heavily involved in a conflict over this issue. Several important battles of the Civil War were fought here. New industries grew during and after the war.

At the turn of the century, Missouri's state government became known for its corruption. The progressive movement made an effort to clean it up. The Great Depression hurt the state's economy badly. The administration of President Roosevelt proposed laws which became known as the New Deal; they were designed to solve the problem. Many public projects were built under its programs.

World War II brought much needed employment to the state. Harry S Truman of Independence became President in 1945. In 1965, the Gateway Arch was built in St. Louis as a symbol of Missouri's geographical gateway to the west.

Missouri has over five million people. More than half of them live in the urban areas. Major cities have declined in population since 1970; at the same time, suburbs have grown.
About eleven percent of the state is made up of minority ethnic groups. The state is considered to be part of the Bible Belt but has a large Catholic population. People are employed in many different ways, including manufacturing, tourism, agriculture, and mining.

Tourists get a bat's-eye view of one of the hundreds of caves to be explored in Missouri.

REVIEW

1. Write a brief definition for each of the terms listed at the beginning of the chapter under "Terms to Look For."
2. Make a list of the important geographic features in Missouri. Include their location.
3. Identify two or three important things about each of the four geographic regions of the state.
4. Why is Missouri's climate called "mild"?
5. Describe the Indian civilizations that have lived in Missouri.
6. Who were the first settlers in what is now the state of Missouri?
7. Why was Missouri called the "jumping off place"?
8. How was Missouri involved in the Civil War?
9. What influence did the progressive movement have on the state?
10. List at least ten facts that describe the people of Missouri today.

INVESTIGATE

At the end of each chapter in this book you will be asked to keep a file of facts about Missouri. You will have to look up these facts outside of your textbook. The facts to look up will be listed under "Facts and Figures File" in the column called INVESTIGATE. These facts will be basic information that will help you to be an effective citizen. You are encouraged to add more facts to your file and share them with other students.

Facts and Figures File:
Make a list of the major characteristics of the state of Missouri. Topics you should include are: people, geography, economy, politicians, history, buildings, and culture.

Make a list of the major employers in the state. Beside each employer, list what the employer makes or does, and where it is located.

PROJECT

Make a timeline for the history of Missouri. Use a large sheet of butcher paper or several notebook sheets taped together.

Draw a thick horizontal line and short vertical lines on both ends. Start with 500 B.C. on the far left, and end with 2004 on the far right. In between, write the important events in Missouri's history in the order in which they happened. Include the date for each event. Draw a vertical line through your timeline at the date on which the event occurred.

Your timeline might be a longer version of something like this:

500 B.C. —————————— 2004 A. D.

POINT/COUNTERPOINT

Many states, including Missouri, try to attract new industry. Some people, however, believe that the growth of industry in the state will do more harm than good.

Research the subject of more growth. Go to your library, talk to people in business, labor leaders, farmers, and environmental groups. Choose whether you are for or against more growth and write an essay in support of your position. Include as many facts as you can. With a class partner, present your arguments to the rest of your class.

TERMS TO LOOK FOR

- law
- representatives
- legislature
- General Assembly
- direct democracy
- bicameral
- House of Representatives
- Senate
- unicameral
- constitutional qualifications
- political qualifications
- availability
- term
- session
- districts
- reapportionment
- one man-one vote
- gerrymandering
- speaker
- leader
- whip
- caucus
- ex-officio
- majority party
- minority party
- president of the Senate
- president pro tempore
- bills
- standing committees
- joint committee
- seniority
- chairperson
- hearings
- amendments
- pigeon holing
- perfection calendar
- perfected
- committee of the whole
- voice vote
- roll call vote
- conference committee
- veto
- override
- initiative
- referendum

2

Missouri Government: The Legislative Branch

One of government's biggest jobs is making laws. A *law* is a rule about what may or may not be done by people. The last time you read a newspaper or watched the news on television, you probably saw examples of laws in our state. We have laws about crimes, taxes, schools, health, and many other things. In a democracy, the people can control the laws that are made. This is most often done by electing ***representatives*** who write and approve the laws. Sometimes the people themselves can vote on a law, though it is not practical to do so in most cases. State laws concern the health, welfare, and safety of all the people in the state. In Missouri, laws may be made in two ways. Most laws are made by the ***legislature.*** The legislature is the lawmaking branch of government called the *General Assembly.* Its members are elected by the voters to be representatives of the people. The other lawmaking method is called ***direct democracy,*** which allows the people to vote on laws in two ways called initiative and referendum. Making laws involves much discussion among representatives. Many groups try to influence the legislature. In this chapter you will learn what the legislative branch of government in Missouri is, and how it works. You will also learn about direct democracy.

Two Ways to Make Laws

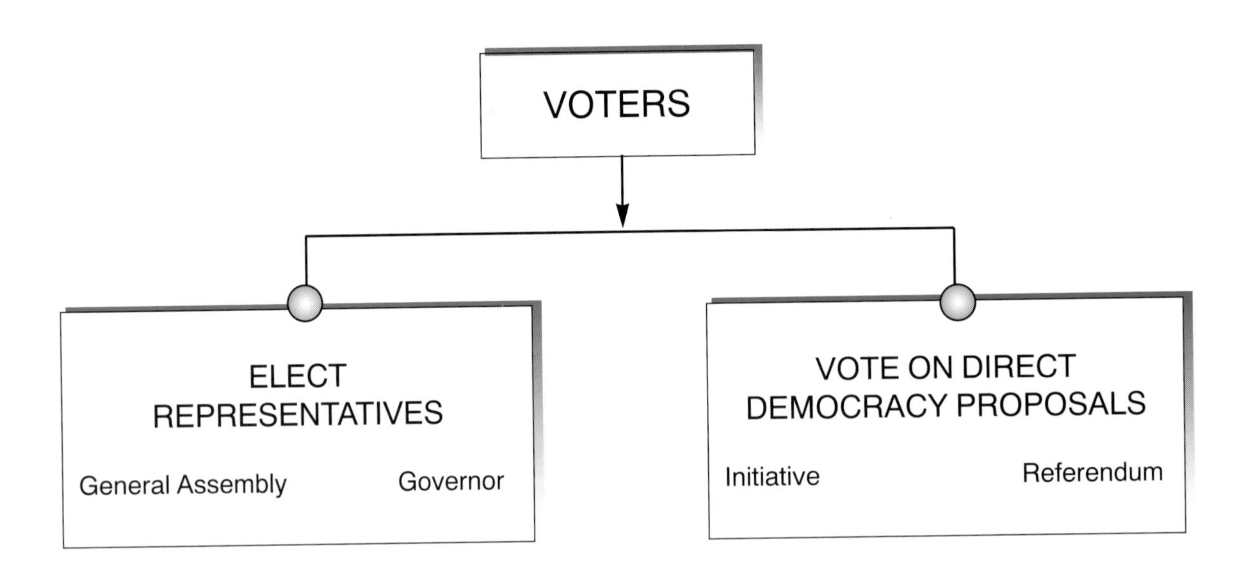

THE GENERAL ASSEMBLY

Missouri has a ***bicameral*** legislature. Bicameral means that the legislature is divided into two houses called the ***House of Representatives*** and the ***Senate.*** There are 163 members in the House of Representatives and 34 in the Senate.

The House of Representatives is often called "the House." The House and the Senate are collectively called "the houses" of the General Assembly. Members of the House and Senate are chosen by the voters. All other states, except Nebraska, also have bicameral legislatures. Nebraska has only one house in its legislature, making it a ***unicameral*** legislature.

Having two houses means that each law will be considered twice. Each house acts as a "check and balance" on the other. This allows all ideas to be considered before any law is made.

WHAT WOULD CHANGE IF MISSOURI HAD A UNICAMERAL LEGISLATURE?

HOW ARE THE REASONS FOR HAVING A BICAMERAL LEGISLATURE IN MISSOURI DIFFERENT FROM THE REASONS FOR HAVING A BICAMERAL CONGRESS FOR THE NATIONAL GOVERNMENT?

Qualifications

The Missouri constitution requires different qualifications to be a member of the House of Representatives or the Senate. A qualification is something that must be true of a person to be elected. Some of the required ***constitutional qualifications*** for the House are:

1. A member must be at least 24 years old.
2. A member must be a registered voter for at least two years.
3. A member must have lived in the district from which he or she is elected for at least one year.

The constitutional qualifications for the Senate are:

1. A member must be at least 30 years old.
2. A member must be a registered voter for at least three years.
3. A member must have lived in the district from which he or she is elected for at least one year.

A prospective candidate for either house must get signatures of registered voters on petitions, which are then presented to the secretary of state's office. If there are enough valid signatures on the petitions, the candidate's name will then be placed on the ballot.

Unwritten ***political qualifications*** are also important. These are traits that are typical of winning candidates for the General Assembly. Some of these political qualifications are:

1. Most candidates who win elections are either Democrats or Republicans. These are the two main parties in the state and in the nation. Political parties are groups that share basic ideas. Each party tries to gets its candidates elected to office.
2. Many winning candidates in Missouri are called "conservative." This means that they do not like to make changes quickly. They are cautious about spending money. They oppose many government programs.
3. A candidate must be able to raise enough money for his or her campaign.

The three branches of Missouri state government are located in Jefferson City's state capitol complex, shown here. The first state capitol was located in St. Charles from 1821 to 1828.

Campaigns are very expensive because of the high cost of using television, radio, and other highly visible ways to advertise.

4. ***Availability*** is something else people look for, something personal or familiar about the candidate. Winners are usually married and have children, attend church regularly, and own their own homes. Their names are generally already well known by the public.

Q:

HOW ARE THE QUALIFICATIONS FOR OUR LEGISLATURE DIFFERENT FROM THOSE FOR CONGRESS?

DISCUSSION: IF YOU COULD CHANGE THE QUALIFICATIONS FOR MEMBERS OF THE GENERAL ASSEMBLY, WHAT CHANGES WOULD YOU MAKE? WHY?

WHICH ARE MORE IMPORTANT TO A CANDIDATE, CONSTITUTIONAL OR POLITICAL QUALIFICATIONS?

EXPLAIN THE IDEA OF "POLITICAL QUALIFICATIONS" IN YOUR OWN WORDS.

Membership

Most members of the General Assembly today are men. Many come from the rural areas of the state. Most are farmers, small businessmen, or lawyers. Most members of the General Assembly must earn money in addition to their income of $24,313 per year for being a member. Anyone who works for the national, state, or city government may not become a member of the General Assembly.

Most members of the General Assembly are elected for more than one term This results in a small change in the actual members of the General Assembly. A member may leave office for one of three reasons:

1. The member is defeated in an election.
2. The member retires.
3. The boundaries of the district from which a member was elected are changed.

Comparison of the House and Senate

CHARACTERISTIC	House	Senate
Number of members	163	34
Constitutional qualifications	Age 24 Registered voter 2 years District resident 1 year	Age 30 Registered voter 3 years District resident 1 year
Term	Two years	Four years
Elected from	House districts	Senate districts
Presiding officer	Speaker	President President pro tempore

Q:

HOW DO YOU THINK THE MEMBERSHIP OF THE LEGISLATURE WOULD CHANGE IF MEMBERS WERE PAID A HIGHER SALARY?

DISCUSSION: WHAT IS THE EFFECT ON THE GENERAL ASSEMBLY OF THE FACT THAT FEW REPRESENTATIVES ARE NEW AFTER EACH ELECTION?

Term and Session

The General Assembly's regular session begins on the first Wednesday of January following each general election. Members of the House of Representatives are elected for two-year terms. Members of the Senate are elected for four-year terms.

The General Assembly's regular ***session*** begins on the first Wednesday of January following each general election. The constitution requires the General Assembly to adjourn on May 30 each year. Special sessions may be called at other times by the governor. With a three-fourths vote in both houses, members of the General Assembly may call themselves into special session. Special sessions are often called to work on a specific issue.

DISCUSSION: WHAT IS AN ADVANTAGE OF HAVING A DIFFERENT TERM IN THE HOUSE COMPARED TO THE SENATE? A DISADVANTAGE?

Election of Members

Members of the General Assembly are elected from ***districts.*** A district is an area from which one person is elected. The districts from which House members are elected are different from those of Senate members. Each House district has about the same number of people living in it. The same is true of each Senate district. House and Senate districts have different boundaries.

A census is taken every ten years by the United States government. This is done at the beginning of each decade (1970, 1980, 1990, etc.). In Missouri, a commission is appointed after every census to redraw district boundary lines. Changing boundary lines is called ***reapportionment.***

In 1964, the U.S. Supreme Court ordered that each district for the House or the Senate should have about the same number of people in it. This is the principle of ***"one man–one vote."*** The commission must follow the one man–one vote idea when it redraws district boundary lines. For example, the 1980 census showed that the city of St. Louis had lost population. As a result, St. Louis had fewer members of the General Assembly.

District boundary lines may also be drawn for political advantage. This is called ***gerrymandering.*** There are two reasons for gerrymandering. One is to put the other party's voters in one area; another is to create a district which has a small majority of your own party's voters. Gerrymandering may be illegal if it can be proven.

The winner in an election is the person with the most votes. It does not matter whether the winner has one more vote than his/her opponent, or all of the votes in the district. How people in an area may vote can often be predicted by past voting and by how they are registered.

There are 163 House districts set by law. This number is divided into the total population of the state. The result is the number of people that should be in each House district. No district may have fewer than three-fourths of this number. Also, no district may have more than five-fourths of this number. Therefore, each member of the House represents close to the same number of people.

There are 34 members of the Senate. The same system is used to decide the number of people in each Senate district. Each Senate district has more people in it than a House district. This is because there are fewer members of the Senate. Direct democracy may not be used to change this process.

Candidates for the General Assembly from each party are nominated at a primary election. This election takes place before the general elections. Members of the House are elected every two years at the general election in November. Senators are elected every other general election.

> **Q:**
>
> WHAT IS THE DIFFERENCE BETWEEN "REAPPORTIONMENT" AND "GERRYMANDERING"?

DISCUSSION: WHY DO YOU THINK THE SUPREME COURT MADE THE "ONE MAN-ONE VOTE" RULING?

RESEARCH: USING MAPS SHOWING MISSOURI'S LEGISLATIVE DISTRICTS TWENTY YEARS AGO AND TODAY, IDENTIFY THE AREAS OF THE STATE THAT HAVE GAINED AND LOST MEMBERS OF THE GENERAL ASSEMBLY.

LEADERSHIP

House of Representatives

The presiding officer of the House is called the ***Speaker of the House.*** The speaker is a member of the House who is elected by the other members. Each political party supports its candidate for speaker. Members usually vote for the candidate

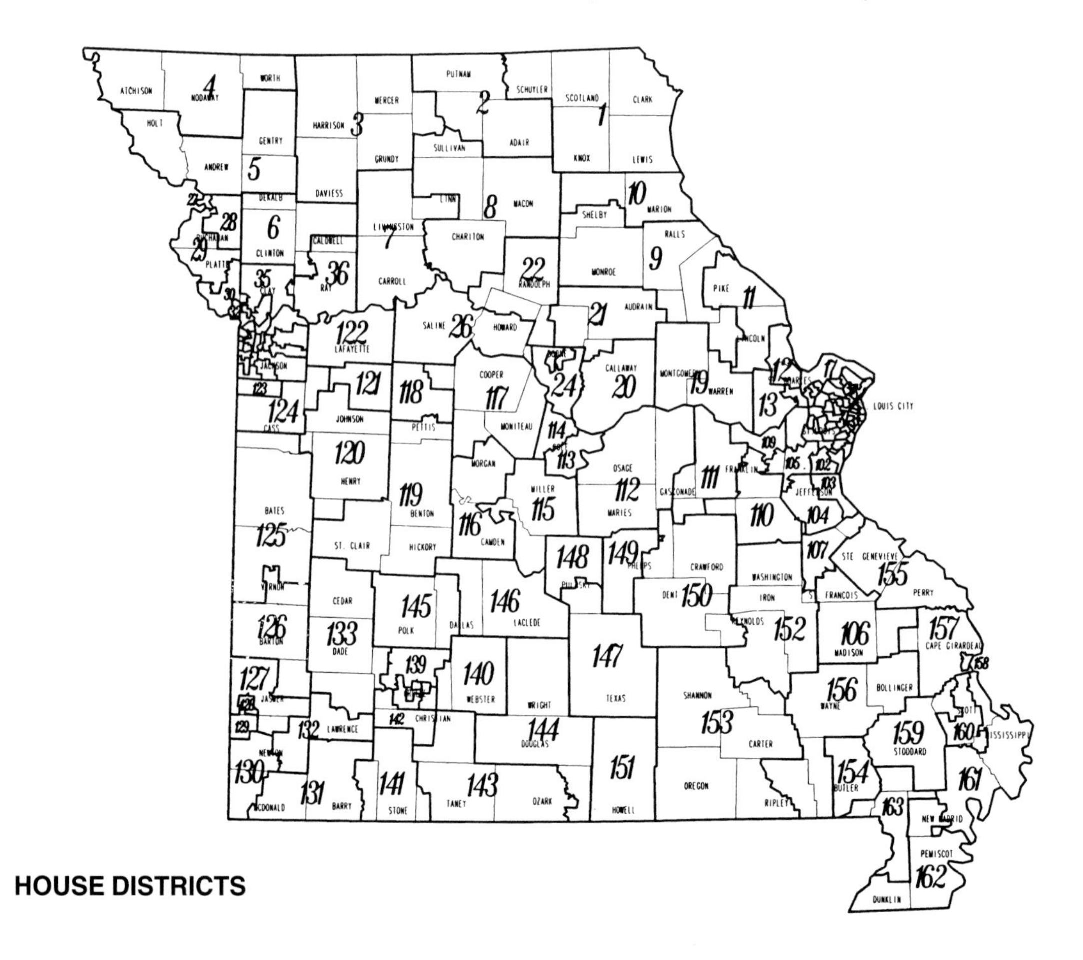

HOUSE DISTRICTS

of their party. This means that the party with a majority of members controls the speaker's position. The major powers of the speaker are:

1. Calls on members who wish to speak
2. Appoints members of committees
3. Appoints chairpersons of committees
4. Assigns proposals for laws (bills) to committees
5. Rules a member "out of order" for not following the rules of the House

The House also elects a speaker pro tempore to take the place of the speaker when he or she is not available.

Each political party has its own leaders. Each party in the House chooses a ***leader*** and a ***whip.*** This is done by each party in a party ***caucus.*** The party caucus is a meeting of all House members from a political party. The Democratic caucus chooses the Democratic party's leader and whip; the Republican caucus chooses its leader and whip. Each caucus also may decide on what proposals it will try to make into law.

The job of a party leader is to get the House to pass the proposals supported by that party. The leader tries to keep the support of his or her own party members and win support from the other party. The party leader is also an ***ex-officio*** member of all committees. Ex-officio means "because of one's office"; therefore, the party leader is also on every committee.

The party whip helps the leader to get and keep support for the party's programs. Most members of the General Assembly, however, are more concerned about their own districts than about what their party wants. This makes the job of party leader very difficult.

The ***majority party*** is the political party with more than half of the members of the House. The leader and whip of the majority party are called the "majority leader" and "majority whip." The other party is the ***minority party.*** Its leaders are called the "minority leader" and "minority whip."

Leadership in the General Assembly

HOUSE	SENATE
Speaker	President
Speaker Pro Tempore	President Pro Tempore
Majority Leader	Majority Leader
Majority Whip	Majority Whip
Minority Leader	Minority Leader
Minority Whip	Minority Whip
Majority Caucus	Majority Caucus
Minority Caucus	Minority Caucus
Committee Chairpersons	Committee Chairpersons

Q:

WHAT IS THE JOB OF EACH OF THE LEADERSHIP POSITIONS IN THE HOUSE?

WHAT POWER DOES THE PARTY CAUCUS HOLD IN THE HOUSE?

DISCUSSION: WHY DOES THE MAJORITY PARTY NEED LEADERS IF IT HAS MORE THAN HALF OF THE MEMBERS IN THE HOUSE?

Senate

The presiding officer of the Senate is called its president. The state's lieutenant governor is the ex-officio ***president of the Senate.*** He or she simply calls on members who wish to speak, and may vote only in case of a tie.

The Senate elects a ***president pro tempore.*** This person acts as a presiding officer when the lieutenant governor is absent. The president pro tempore appoints chairpersons and members of committees in the Senate. He or she also assigns bills to committees for study.

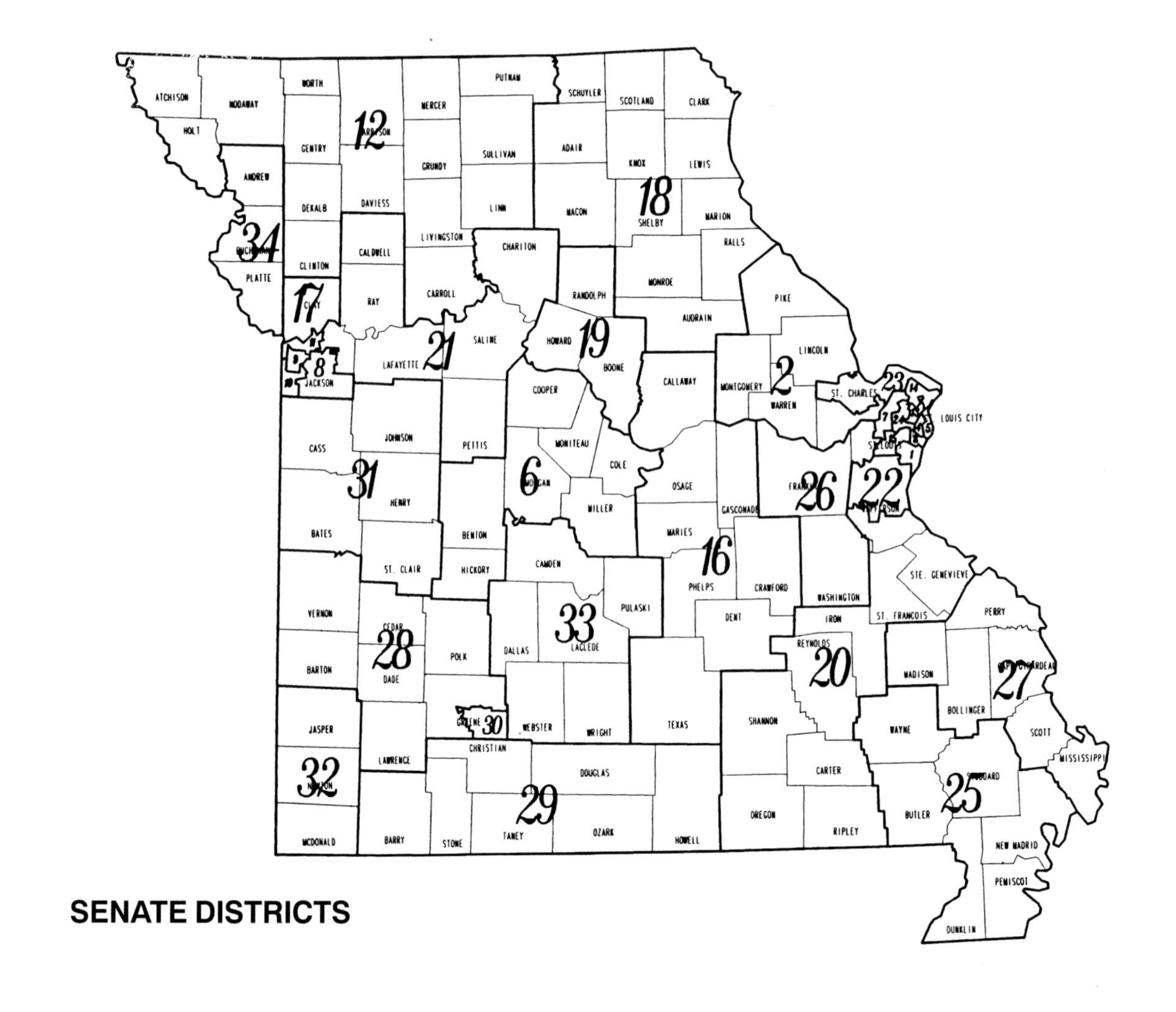

SENATE DISTRICTS

The walls of the Senate Chamber (shown here) of the Missouri Capitol building are inscribed with such political philosophies as"Nothing is politically right that is morally wrong" and "Free and fair discussion will ever be found the firmest friend to truth."

The Senate has majority and minority parties like the House. It also has party leaders and party whips. Their jobs are the same as in the House, with one exception. The majority leader of the Senate also sets the schedule and order of business in the Senate. There is also a caucus system for each political party, as is in the House.

Q:

HOW IS THE ORGANIZATION OF THE SENATE DIFFERENT FROM THE HOUSE? HOW IS IT THE SAME?

WHY ARE THE SPEAKER AND THE PRESIDENT PRO TEMPORE VERY POWERFUL OFFICIALS?

THE COMMITTEE SYSTEM

A system of committees is used in each house. These committees study all proposed laws, called ***bills.*** Committees are organized by the subjects of the bills that they consider, such as urban affairs, agriculture, and education. These committees are called ***standing committees*** because they exist year after year. Each member of the House and Senate is on one or more committees. Bills are sent to committees for study, based on their subjects. This system divides the hundreds of bills so they can be studied carefully.

Another type of committee is a ***joint committee.*** It has members from both the House and the Senate. Joint committees are often used to get information on controversial issues. An example of this type of committee is the Medical Malpractice Committee.

The speaker appoints committee members for the House. The president pro tempore does this job in the Senate. Each committee in the House has about the same percent of each party's members as in the whole House. The same is true in the Senate. Therefore, the majority party has a majority of its members on committees. Members who have seniority are more likely to be put on committees they want. ***Seniority*** is the length of time a person has been a member.

Each committee also has a ***chairperson*** who is chosen by the speaker in the House or the president pro tempore in the Senate. The chairperson is also likely to be a member of the majority party. Among the many jobs the chairperson may have are:

- decide which bills will be studied from those sent to the committee.
- call on members who want to speak.
- maintain order.
- guide bills from the committee in debate.

Q:

WHY IS THE COMMITTEE SYSTEM USED IN THE GENERAL ASSEMBLY?

DISCUSSION: WHAT ARE THE ADVANTAGES OR POWERS THAT THE COMMITTEE SYSTEM GIVES TO THE MAJORITY PARTY?

The Tenth Amendment to the United States Constitution reads:

"The powers not delegated to the United States by the Constitution nor prohibited by it to the States, are reserved to the States respectively, or to the people."

This statement means that the states have those powers which are not given to the national government by the United States Constitution. There has long been a debate about what those powers are. The national government's powers are worded in a very general way.

For example, Congress has the power to tax and spend for the "general welfare." The courts have said that these national government powers include many things which were once thought to be only state powers. The result is that the states are less able to make laws on some subjects than they were many years ago.

Article III of the Missouri state constitution says that the General Assembly shall make all state laws. The subject of these laws is most often the health, safety, or welfare of the citizens. For example, the General Assembly has made laws about such subjects as:

- crimes, like arson, burglary, and theft
- traffic regulations
- education
- health standards for restaurants
- building roads and bridges
- help for the poor and unemployed

The state constitution also limits the power of the General Assembly: no special or local laws can be made relative to certain subjects. Laws have to apply to all people in the state. Another limit is that the General Assembly may not move the state capitol away from Jefferson City.

RESEARCH: FIND OUT WHAT SUBJECTS OF LAWS ARE LIMITED OR INFLUENCED BY THE NATIONAL GOVERNMENT. (ONE EXAMPLE IS THE 55 MILES-PER-HOUR SPEED LIMIT ON STATE TWO-LANE HIGHWAYS.)

WITH A PARTNER: MAKE A LIST OF OTHER SUBJECTS ABOUT WHICH THE GENERAL ASSEMBLY MAY MAKE LAWS.

MISSOURI HOUSE OF REPRESENTATIVES
92nd General Assembly, 1st Regular Session
Standing, Statutory, and Special Committees

Administration and Accounts, *Standing*
Agriculture, *Standing*
Appropriations - Agriculture and Natural Resources, *Standing*
Appropriations - Education, *Standing*
Appropriations - General Administration, *Standing*
Appropriations - Health, Mental Health and Social Services, *Standing*
Appropriations - Public Safety and Corrections, *Standing*
Appropriations - Transportation and Economic Development, *Standing*
Budget, *Standing*
Children and Families, *Standing*
Communications, Energy, and Technology, *Standing*
Conservation and Natural Resources, *Standing*
Corrections and State Institutions, *Standing*
Crime Prevention and Public Safety, *Standing*
Education, *Standing*
Elections, *Standing*
Ethics, *Standing*
Financial Services, *Standing*
Health Care Policy, *Standing*
Homeland Security and Veterans Affairs, *Standing*
Job Creation and Economic Development, *Standing*
Joint Advisory Committee on Tobacco Securitization, *Statutory*
Joint Committee on Administrative Rules, *Statutory*
Joint Committee on Capital Improvements and Leases Oversight, *Statutory*
Joint Committee on Corrections, *Statutory*
Joint Committee on Court Automation, *Statutory*
Joint Committee on Economic Development, Policy & Planning, *Statutory*
Joint Committee on Education, *Statutory*
Joint Committee on Gaming and Wagering, *Statutory*
Joint Committee on Health Care Policy and Planning, *Statutory*
Joint Committee on Legislative Research, *Statutory*
Joint Committee on Public Employee Retirement, *Statutory*
Joint Committee on Terrorism, Bioterrorism, and Homeland Security, *Statutory*
Joint Committee on Transportation Oversight, *Statutory*
Joint Committee on Wetlands, *Statutory*
Judiciary, *Standing*
Legislative Research, Oversight Subcommittee, *Statutory*
Local Government, *Standing*
Professional Registration and Licensing, *Standing*
Retirement, *Standing*
Rules, *Standing*
Senior Security, *Standing*
Small Business, *Standing*
Special Committee on General Laws, *Special*
Special Committee on Bonding Authority, *Special*
Special Committee on Urban Issues, *Special*
Tax Policy, *Standing*
Tourism and Cultural Affairs, *Standing*
Transportation and Motor Vehicles, *Standing*
Workforce Development and Workplace Safety, *Standing*

HOW THE GENERAL ASSEMBLY MAKES LAWS

Most state laws are made by the General Assembly. A law must be approved in the same form by both the House and the Senate. Also, the governor must either approve or disapprove the law.

Remember that a proposed law is called a "bill." There are eight basic steps to the making of a law. These steps are outlined on pages 28 and 29. Both houses of the General Assembly follow steps 1 through 5 separately.

STEP 1: INTRODUCTION

A bill may be written by a member of the General Assembly with the help of the staff. It may also be prepared by the governor's office. It may be suggested by an interest group, such as a farmers' group, medical association, retail stores' group, or citizens' group.

A bill must be introduced into either house by a member of that house. That member becomes its sponsor. Bills may start in either house, but must be about only one subject. When a bill is introduced, it is given its first reading, a title, and a number. After copies of the bill are printed, it is given a second reading.

STEP 2: COMMITTEE ACTION

The speaker of the House and president pro tempore of the Senate send proposed bills to standing committees in their respective houses based on their subjects. The job of the committee is to study and discuss the bill in detail. The committee will invite people who support and oppose the bill to express their opinions about the bill. This is done at scheduled meetings called ***hearings.***

Hearings are usually open to the public. The purpose of hearings is to get information which the committee will then discuss. Changes may be made in the bill at this time. Such changes are called ***amendments.*** The committee may even write a whole new bill, which would be called a "substitute bill." However, this does not allow the bill to be changed from its original intent.

Some committees are divided into smaller groups called subcommittees. Subcommittees are used when a committee has a large number of bills to study.

After study, the committee makes a recommendation to the full house. It may recommend that the bill be approved, or not approved. A bill may die in committee because it is not "reported out" of committee. This is called ***pigeon holing.*** Pigeon holing means that the committee takes no action at all on the bill. If a bill is pigeon holed, a vote of one-third of the house can take it away from the committee.

STEP 3: CALENDAR

The bill is placed on the list of bills to be considered by the full house. This list is called the ***perfection calendar.*** The speaker and president pro tempore place bills on the calendar for their respective houses. Bills from the minority party often are heard last.

STEP 4: FLOOR DEBATE

The bill as reported by the committee is now debated by the full house. A meeting of all the members of an entire house is call the ***committee of the whole.*** The bill may be amended on the floor. Amendments are proposed and voted on one at a time. A motion is then made to call the bill ***perfected,*** meaning that there are no more amendments.

This is followed by a ***voice vote,*** where members vote aloud in a chorus for or against a bill. No record is kept of how members voted. Five members may demand a ***roll call vote*** on perfection. Each member may vote "yes" or "no," and a record is kept of how each member voted.

The bill is printed in final form if perfection is approved.

STEP 5: FINAL VOTE

The bill is read a third time. Members may again

speak on the bill if they wish. No major amendments may be made. A roll call vote is always taken on the entire bill as amended.

STEP 6: REFERRAL

If the bill was introduced in the House, it now goes to the Senate. If introduced in the Senate, it goes to the House. If it has already been through both houses, it may go to the governor or to conference committee.

STEP 7: CONFERENCE COMMITTEE

Major bills seldom go through both houses the first time without change. The House and Senate may have different versions of the bill. The bill then goes to ***conference committee.***

The conference committee is made up of members from both houses. They are chosen by the speaker and president pro tempore. The committee must find a compromise on the bill. Then, both houses must vote on the new wording of the bill. They most likely will follow the recommendations of the conference committee.

Missouri Senator William L. Clay (D, Dist. 4/St. Louis) proposes an idea during a discussion in the Senate chambers.

STEP 8: GOVERNOR'S ACTION

The governor may choose to sign or veto the bill. The governor has 15 days to act on the bill during a session of the legislature. An extension of 30 more days is given if the legislature has adjourned or has a long recess.

The bill becomes law if it is signed by the governor. The governor may also ***veto*** the bill. Veto means "I forbid." If the governor does not approve of the law, he can either veto the bill or try to let it die by not signing it.

The General Assembly can, however, still make the bill a law. To do this, each house must again approve the bill with a two-thirds vote. This is called an ***override.*** The General Assembly may pass a joint resolution to make the bill a law if the governor takes no action at all.

The General Assembly also can choose to send a bill to the voters for approval instead of to the governor. This is a form of direct democracy. The voters would then decide whether the bill becomes law at the next election. The governor cannot veto a bill voted on by this process.

Most new laws take effect 90 days after the end of the General Assembly in which they were passed. There are a few exceptions to this rule, such as bills that address spending money, or an emergency. The reasons for the emergency must be explained in the law. The waiting period allows voters to use the referendum process, which is described later in this chapter.

Q:

WHAT IS THE MAIN PURPOSE OF EACH STEP IN THE PROCESS OF MAKING A LAW?

DISCUSSION: HOW IS THE "CHECKS AND BALANCES" SYSTEM BUILT INTO THE PROCESS OF MAKING LAWS?

RESEARCH: WHAT BILLS HAVE BEEN VETOED BY THE GOVERNOR IN THE PAST YEAR? WHAT HAPPENED TO THE BILLS?

How a Bill Becomes a Law

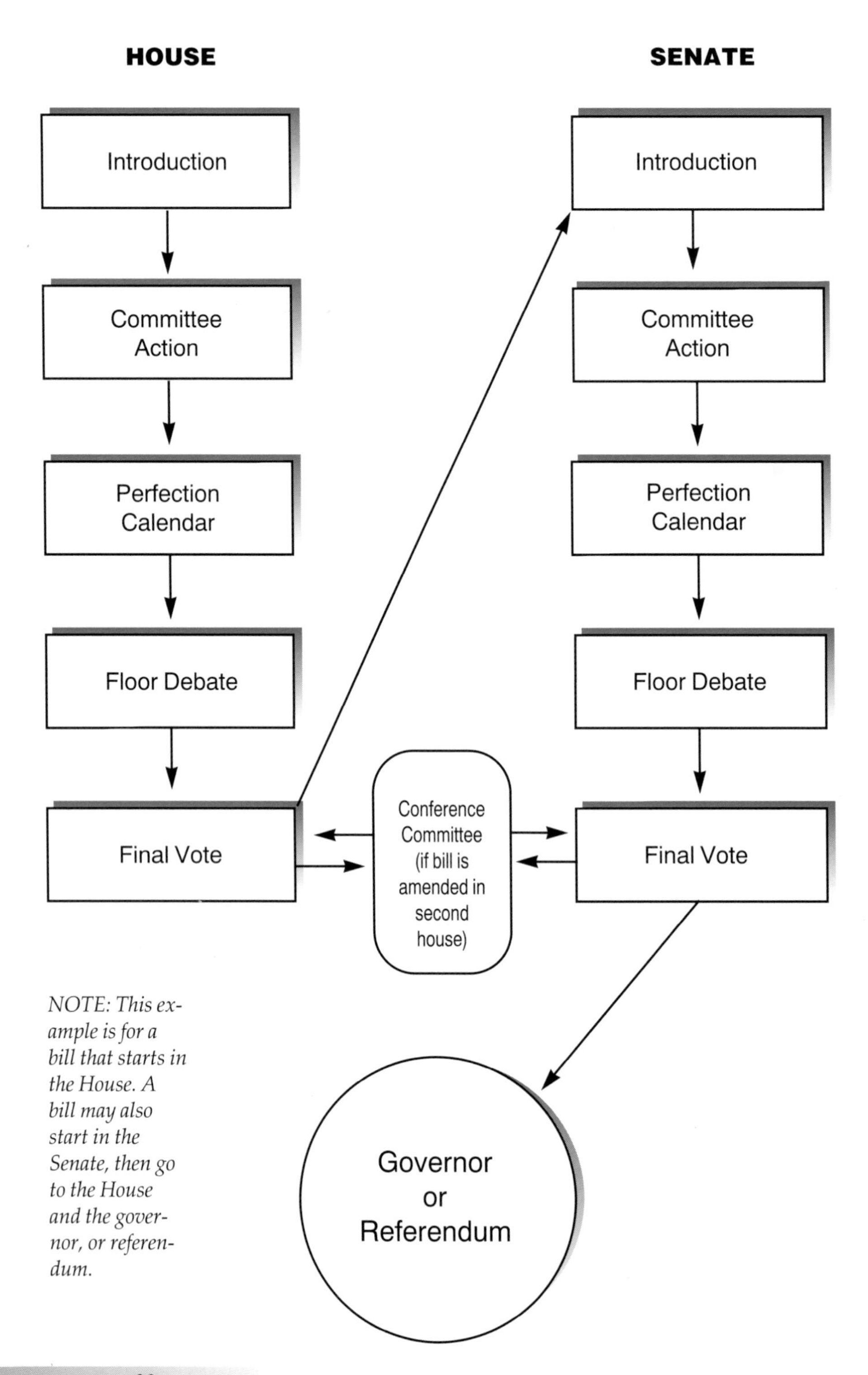

NOTE: This example is for a bill that starts in the House. A bill may also start in the Senate, then go to the House and the governor, or referendum.

Legislators often gather in committee to confer on new bills that are introduced before discussing them on the "floor."

DIRECT DEMOCRACY

At the beginning of this chapter it was mentioned that there are two ways to make laws in Missouri: through the General Assembly, or by a method called direct democracy. Direct democracy is a way to let the people vote directly on a law or change in the state constitution. There are two types of direct democracy: initiative and referendum.

Initiative

Initiative allows the people to vote on one of three things: a change in an old law, a new law, or a change in the state constitution. There are two types of initiative:

1. Constitutional Initiative
   This is a way of placing a proposed change in the state constitution on the ballot for a vote of the people. Such a change is called an amendment. To get the proposed change placed on a ballot, petitions must be signed by registered voters equal to 8 percent of the voters in each of two-thirds of the congressional districts in the state.

   A congressional district is an area that elects a member of the U.S. House of Representatives. There are now nine congressional districts in Missouri. So the number of signatures needed is 8 percent of the voters in six congressional districts.

   The petitions must include the wording of the proposed amendment and they must be filed with the secretary of state at least four months before the election. A constitutional amendment may be about only one subject.

2. Statutory Initiative
   This process allows a new law or change in an old law to be proposed and voted on by the people. It is called "statutory" because laws are also called "statutes."

   Again, petitions must be signed by registered voters to place the proposal on the ballot. The number of signatures needed for a statutory initiative, however, is 5 percent of the voters in two-thirds of the congressional districts. All other rules for a statutory initiative are the same as for a constitutional initiative.

   The initiative will be placed on the next general election ballot. Voters may vote "yes" or "no" on the issue. It is approved if more than half of those voting vote "yes." If fewer than half approve, the initiative dies.

   It is also possible that two initiatives disagree with one another. If both are approved, the one with the most "yes" votes goes into effect.

Referendum

Referendum is a way for voters to review a law after the legislature has approved it. Referendum means that the law is referred to the people for their approval before the law goes into effect. There are three types of referendum.

1. Constitutional Referendum
   An amendment to the state constitution that is proposed by the General Assembly must be approved by the people. It is placed on the ballot. A majority of those voting on it decide if it is approved.
2. Legislative Referendum
   Laws are made by the General Assembly and may be sent to the governor or to the voters for approval.

KIND OF DIRECT DEMOCRACY	TYPE	PURPOSE	SIGNATURES NEEDED
INITIATIVE	Constitutional	People place amendment to the state constitution on the ballot for a vote	8% of voters in two-thirds of the congressional districts
	Statutory	People place a change in the state law on the ballot for a vote	5% of voters in two-thirds of the congressional districts
REFERENDUM	Constitutional	Legislature places a constitutional amendment on the ballot for approval by the people	None
	Legislative	Legislature places a new law on the ballot for approval by the people instead of sending it to the governor	None
	Popular	People demand to vote on law approved by the legislature	5% of voters in two-thirds of the congressional districts

Legislative referendum is when the final bill is sent to the voters. The bill is placed on the ballot for a vote of the people. Again, a majority of those voting decide if the bill is approved. This may be done for controversial issues. It may also be done when the General Assembly knows that the governor will veto the bill.

3. Popular Referendum
   This process forces a law already approved by the General Assembly and the governor to be put on the ballot for a vote of the people. A law made by the General Assembly does not go into effect until 90 days after the end of the session in which it was passed.

   Popular referendum is used by having petitions signed by registered voters. The number of signatures needed is 5 percent of the voters in each of two-thirds of the state's congressional districts. In Missouri, this is 5 percent of the voters in six congressional districts.

   The petitions must be filed with the secretary of state within the 90-day waiting period. The bill becomes law if more than half of those voting approve it.

   Referendum cannot be used against some kinds of laws. These include laws

   - needed to keep the peace.
   - for health and safety.
   - that spend money to run state government.
   - for maintaining state institutions.
   - regarding money for public schools.

The governor may not veto any bill that the people have approved by initiative or referendum. The people vote on bills in the general elections, but the General Assembly may also order a special election.

OFFICIAL BALLOT

STATE OF MISSOURI
SPECIAL ELECTION, TUESDAY, APRIL 7, 1987

STATUTORY MEASURE

PROPOSITION A

(Referendum ordered by the 84th General Assembly) (First Regular Session)

YES ☐

NO ☐

Provides for repair and replacement of bridges, provides highway and safety improvements by increasing fees on larger trucks, limiting road fund administrative costs, and supplementing motor fuel user fees by four cents per gallon. Provides estimated one hundred one million dollars for state road and bridge system, nineteen million dollars for city street improvements, and thirteen million dollars for county roads and bridges.

INSTRUCTIONS TO VOTERS

If you are in favor of this statutory measure, place an X in the box opposite "YES".
If you are opposed to this statutory measure, place an X in the box opposite "NO".

INSTRUCTIONS TO VOTERS
(Punch Card)

If you are in favor of this statutory measure, punch a hole opposite the word "YES".
If you are opposed to this statutory measure, punch a hole opposite the word "NO".

INSTRUCTIONS TO VOTERS
(Optical Scan)

If you are in favor of this statutory measure, darken the space opposite the word "YES".
If you are opposed to this statutory measure, darken the space opposite the word "NO".

Forms of Direct Democracy

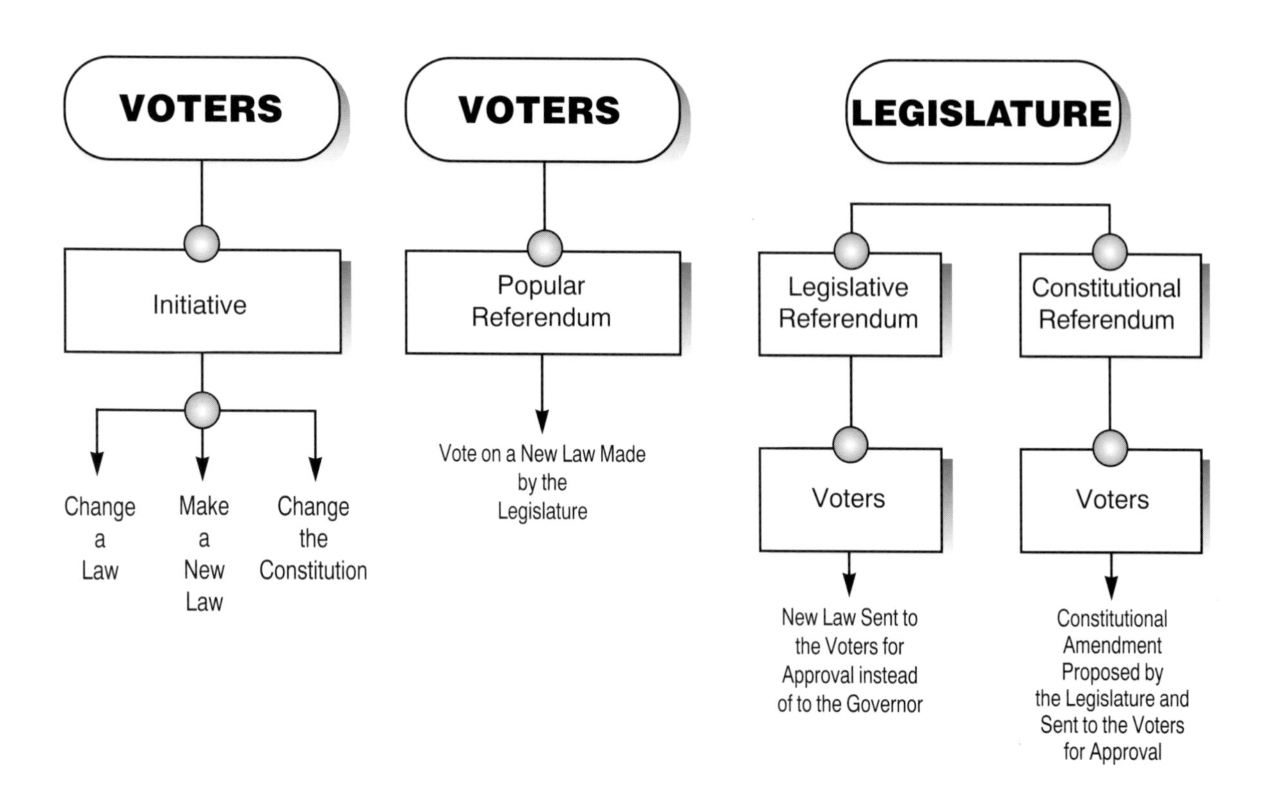

Q:

WHAT ARE THE DIFFERENCES BETWEEN INITIATIVE AND REFERENDUM?

HOW MANY SIGNATURES ARE NEEDED ON PETITIONS TO USE EACH KIND OF DIRECT DEMOCRACY?

WHEN DO VOTERS HAVE A CHANCE TO VOTE ON THESE ISSUES?

WHEN DOES DIRECT DEMOCRACY TAKE THE PLACE OF THE GENERAL ASSEMBLY? OF THE GOVERNOR?

RESEARCH: EXPLAIN HOW THE PROCESS FOR AMENDING MISSOURI'S CONSTITUTION IS DIFFERENT FROM THAT FOR AMENDING THE UNITED STATES CONSTITUTION.

Looking at Direct Democracy

Direct democracy can give the people more involvement in their government. However, problems can also be created by:

1. Interest group power
   Initiative and referendum are often used by organized groups called ***interest groups*** or "pressure groups." Getting the necessary signatures requires the work of many people, who often are paid to collect them.
   Additionally, an advertising campaign is begun to make the voters aware of a proposed law. This advertising is very expensive; therefore, it takes a lot of money and / or many volunteers to get a law on the ballot and approved. Interest groups try to

get laws approved that will benefit their supporters.

2. Lack of voter awareness
   Many people vote for candidates, but not for direct democracy proposals. Often fewer than half of the voters will decide an issue. Some people do not vote on these issues because they do not understand them. Others have not heard of the proposals, and still others will not vote on an issue if it does not affect them.
3. No possible compromise
   Voters must vote either "yes" or "no" on an issue. No compromise is possible between different points of view. Those who put the issue on the ballot either win or lose.

   Bills that go through the General Assembly have a chance to be changed because legislators with different points of view have learned to compromise in order to make a bill acceptable.

Direct democracy can act as a safety valve for people to get what they want. It also has become a chance for special interest groups to get what they want.

The best protection against a bad idea is the public itself. Voters need to pay attention to the issues. They need to find out what is happening in their state and federal governments, and then be sure to vote on the issues as well as for the candidates.

DISCUSSION: ARE THE ADVANTAGES OF DIRECT DEMOCRACY GREATER THAN THE POSSIBLE DISADVANTAGES? HOW?

WHAT CONSTITUTIONAL RIGHTS ARE NEEDED TO USE DIRECT DEMOCRACY EFFECTIVELY?

❐ SUMMARY

The legislative branch of government makes the laws. In Missouri, laws may be made by the General Assembly or by direct democracy. The General Assembly is made up of people who are elected to represent the voters. It has two houses: the House of Representatives and the Senate. Both houses use the same basic rules in making laws.

Most of the work on proposed laws is done by committees. This is followed by debate and the vote of all members of each house. A bill must be approved in the same form by both houses. It is sent for final approval either to the governor or to the people at an election.

Direct democracy is a way to give the people a chance to vote directly on laws. Initiative is used to make laws without the General Assembly. It can also be used to amend the state constitution. Referendum allows the people to vote on a law already approved by the General Assembly.

REVIEW

1. Write a brief definition for each of the terms listed at the beginning of the chapter under "Terms to Look For."
2. Make a list of the constitutional and political qualifications required to be a member of the General Assembly.
3. How long do members of the General Assembly serve in office?
4. Describe how members of the House of Representatives and the Senate in the General Assembly are elected.
5. Make a list of the leaders in the General Assembly and the jobs done by each.
6. What is the role of the committee system in the General Assembly?
7. Explain why the General Assembly cannot make any laws that it wishes.
8. Explain the purpose of each step in making a law.
9. Suppose you oppose a law just made by the General Assembly. How could you use the referenda process against it?
10. Explain the two types of initiative and three kinds of referendum.
11. Looking back at Chapter 1, how do each of the following affect the kinds of laws that are made in Missouri?
    - History of the state
    - Types of people in the state
    - Major industries in the state
    - Geography of the state
    - Important groups in the state

INVESTIGATE

Facts and Figures File:

1. Write the names of the state Senator and Representative for the district where you live. Include their district number, political party, committee assignments, and anything for which they have become known in the General Assembly.
2. Who are the leaders in the General Assembly? Include their names, party affiliations, and where they are from.
3. For each of the direct democracy proposals in the last two elections, list
    - the subject of the proposal.
    - whether it was an initiative or referendum
    - the type of initiative or referendum
    - whether it was approved
    - the groups that supported it and the ones that opposed it
4. Find out the major issues in the current (or just past) session of the General Assembly.
    - What are the major bills being debated?
    - How do your Representative and Senator stand on them?

    Clip articles from the newspaper or magazines that discuss these issues.

Note: Sources can include newspapers and publications from the secretary of state's office.

PROJECT

1. Write a newspaper article on one of the current issues being discussed in the General Assembly. Include information about the "five Ws":
   - Who?
   - What?
   - Where?
   - When?
   - Why?
2. Write a letter to the editor about one of the current issues. Identify the issue, take a position, and explain your reasons for it. Have someone else read your letter and give suggestions. Rewrite it, if desirable. Have it read again by a different person for possible further changes.

   Then send your letter to the editor of your local newspaper. Be sure to check regularly to see whether it is published.
3. Draw a poster showing each step of how a bill becomes a law in Missouri. Illustrate the steps in the process. Be sure to include the governor and possible referendum as well as what the General Assembly does. Make the poster clear, colorful, and interesting. Present it to your class and explain how a bill becomes a law.

POINT/COUNTERPOINT

The final part of this chapter was about direct democracy. It has both advantages and disadvantages.

Suppose the General Assembly introduced an amendment to do away with the initiative and referendum. With two or three other students, form a group to campaign for or against this proposal. Write campaign literature explaining your position. Make posters and leaflets. At the end of the campaign period, have your class vote on the issue. Have a class discussion about the issue after the vote.

- Describe your campaign.
- What problems did you have?
- How did you feel about the issue?
- Did you get others to change their minds?
- What was your most successful argument?
- WHAT DID YOU LEARN?

TERMS TO LOOK FOR

- governor
- executive branch
- consecutive
- merit system
- chief executive
- term
- succession
- impeachment
- administrative powers
- appoint
- deficit spending
- liaison
- budget
- revenue
- adjourn
- veto
- appropriation bill
- line item veto
- special session
- military powers
- national guard
- pardon
- reprieve
- commutation
- extradition
- ceremonial
- lieutenant governor
- ombudsman
- secretary of state
- attorney general
- negligent
- damages
- boards and commissions
- advisory opinion
- state auditor
- depositories

3

The Executive Branch

The main job of the executive branch is to carry out the laws that are made by the legislative branch. This branch does the day-to-day work of the state government. It also has the power to make many rules and decisions that affect our lives. The state constitution and laws have created many offices to do this. Each office is given certain powers to act. Together they are called the ***executive branch*** of state government. The executive branch has changed several times. A new constitution was written in 1945 by a constitutional convention. It created most of the current executive offices. An amendment in the 1960s allowed the governor to serve two ***consecutive*** terms. Consecutive means one right after the other. In 1972 another amendment created more changes. The executive branch is allowed no more than 14 departments. There were departments created for consumer affairs, natural resources, transportation, public safety, social services, agriculture, and revenue. Most workers in these departments are part of the ***merit system.*** This means that they cannot be fired for political reasons. There are two departments that are still under the patronage system. Workers in those departments can be hired and fired for political reasons. One of these departments is the department of revenue. It collects taxes and issues auto and driver's licenses. The other is the department of agriculture. The elected governor is the leader of the executive branch. Many of the other executives in Missouri's state government are also elected. They may be from different political parties. It is difficult for the governor to have much control over other elected officers. The result is that the executive branch may be divided instead of working as a whole.

Missouri has six elected executive officers: governor, lieutenant governor, secretary of state, attorney general, treasurer, and auditor. There are also more than 350 boards, commissions, and agencies that have some executive powers. There are other executive departments whose leaders are appointed.

GOVERNOR

The ***governor*** is called the ***chief executive*** of the state. He or she has much less power over Missouri government than the president has over the national government. The attitude of the governor toward the powers of that office is as important as the powers themselves. One governor may be willing to try fewer actions than another governor.

DISCUSSION: HOW CAN THE ATTITUDE OF THE GOVERNOR TOWARD THE POWERS OF OFFICE AFFECT HOW THE GOVERNOR'S JOB IS DONE?

Qualifications

There are three qualifications for governor in the state constitution. They are:

- minimum of 30 years old
- a U.S. citizen for at least 10 years
- live in Missouri for at least 10 years

These are very limited requirements. Few people who want to be governor are kept from running for the office because of these requirements.

It is the "political qualifications" that really determine who will win an election for governor. You will remember that political qualifications were mentioned for members of the General Assembly too. Political qualifications are traits that recent winning candidates for this office often have had. They are not written into law but generally have included the following:

- well known around the state
- able to raise large amounts of money for campaigns
- male
- married, with children
- own a home
- belong to a church
- have support of one of the major political parties
- moderate to conservative on issues
- have support of major interest groups
- not identified with interests disliked by the public

Q:

WHY ARE THE "POLITICAL QUALIFICATIONS" CONSIDERED TO BE SO IMPORTANT?

RESEARCH: HOW DO THE TWO PAST GOVERNORS FIT THE "POLITICAL QUALIFICATIONS" LISTED ABOVE?

THE EXECUTIVE BRANCH OF MISSOURI GOVERNMENT

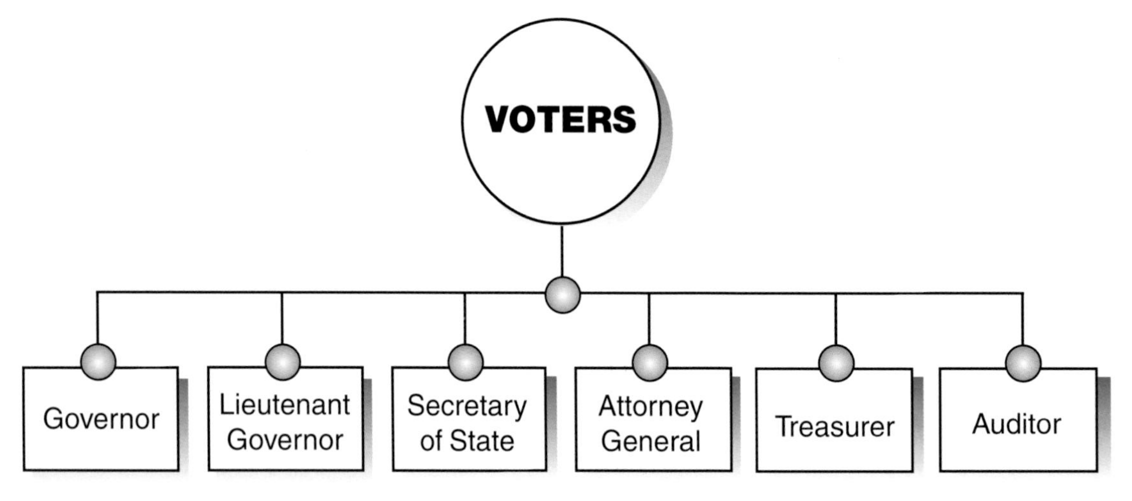

Governor Bob Holden at a press conference discussing the State business.

Term

The executive officers in Missouri are elected at the same time as the President of the United States. The governor is elected to a four-year ***term.*** This means that the governor serves four years in office before the next election. A governor in Missouri may not serve more than two terms. After the amendment allowing governors to serve two consecutive terms, more than likely most will serve two.

Succession

Succession provides for someone to serve as governor if the governor leaves office. This could happen for several reasons. The governor may die, resign, become disabled, or be impeached and removed. If any of these happen in Missouri, the lieutenant governor becomes governor. The lieutenant governor becomes the "acting governor" when the governor is out of the state.

The succession law also names the official who may become governor after the lieutenant governor. This is needed in case the lieutenant governor becomes governor and then dies, resigns, or is removed. The same is true for the next office, and the next, and so forth. This is called the "line of succession."

The proper order of the officials who may succeed to the governor's job after the lieutenant governor is:

1. president pro tempore of the senate
2. speaker of the house
3. secretary of state
4. state auditor
5. state treasurer
6. attorney general

Governors of Missouri

Name	Political Party	Year Elected
Alexander McNair	Democrat	1820
Frederick Bates	Democrat	1824
Abraham Williams	Democrat	President of Senate*
John Miller	Democrat	1825 (special election
John Miller	Democrat	1828
Daniel Dunklin	Democrat	1832
Lilburn Boggs	Democrat	Lt. Governor*
Thomas Reynolds	Democrat	1840
Meredith Marmaduke	Democrat	Lt. Governor*
John Edwards	Democrat	1844
Austin King	Democrat	1848
Sterling Price	Democrat	1852
Trusten Polk	Democrat	1856
Hancock Jackson	Democrat	Lt. Governor*
Robert Stewart	Democrat	1857
Claiborne Jackson	Democrat	1860
Hamilton Gamble	Unionist	1861 (by state convention)
Willard Hall	Unionist	Lt. Governor*
Thomas Fletcher	Republican	1864
Joseph McClurg	Republican	1868
Benjamin Brown	Republican	1870
Silas Woodson	Democrat	1872
Charles Hardin	Democrat	1874
John Phelps	Democrat	1876
Thomas Crittenden	Democrat	1880
John Marmaduke	Democrat	1884
Albert Morehouse	Democrat	Lt. Governor*

*Inherited governorship, rather than elected.

Continued on page 43

Impeachment

The governor and other elected executive officers can be removed by ***impeachment.*** This means that charges are brought against the governor by the House of Representatives.

Impeachment of a governor is tried before a special commission of judges chosen by the Senate. The same process is used for the impeachment of a member of the state supreme court. The impeachment of any other official is tried before the supreme court. The penalty for conviction is removal from office.

Compensation

In 2002 the governor received a salary of $120,086. This amount is determined by law. An extra amount

Governors of Missouri

Name	Political Party	Year Elected
David Francis	Democrat	1888
William Stone	Democrat	1892
Lon Stephens	Democrat	1896
Alexander Dockery	Democrat	1900
Joseph Folk	Democrat	1904
Herbert Hadley	Republican	1908
Elliot Major	Democrat	1912
Frederick Gardner	Democrat	1916
Arthur Hyde	Republican	1920
Sam Baker	Republican	1924
Henry Caulfield	Republican	1928
Guy Park	Democrat	1932
Lloyd Stark	Democrat	1936
Forrest Donnell	Republican	1940
Phil Donnelly	Democrat	1944
Forrest Smith	Democrat	1948
Phil Donnelly	Democrat	1952
James Blair Jr.	Democrat	1956
John Dalton	Democrat	1960
Warren Hearnes	Democrat	1964, 1968**
Christopher Bond	Republican	1972
Joseph Teasdale	Democrat	1976
Christopher Bond	Republican	1980
John Ashcroft	Republican	1984, 1988
Mel Carnahan	Democrat	1992, 1996
Roger Wilson	Democrat	Lt. Governor*
Bob Holden	Democrat	2000

*Inherited governorship, rather than elected.
**First governor to succeed himself because of constitutional change.

of money is allowed for official expenses. The governor has the use of a mansion in Jefferson City and an airplane. He or she also is protected by the Highway Patrol.

Powers

The governor has several powers, some of which are set by the state constitution. Other powers are created by state or national law, or as the result of being chief executive of the state.

1. ***Administrative Powers.*** The governor has the duty to carry out the laws of the state, which is done by directing many officials to actually do the jobs.

A large part of this job involves the power to ***appoint*** officials. The governor appoints the heads of all of the executive departments, who must be confirmed by the Senate. The governor also appoints some department and agency heads who report directly to the governor. They are responsible to the governor for what their department does. The people in these jobs usually change when a new governor is elected. The governor also has the power to remove most of the top appointed officials from their positions.

The majority of state government workers are not appointed by the governor, nor can they be removed by the governor. These people are protected by what is called the merit system, which prevents most state workers from being fired for political reasons. They may be removed from their positions only because their job no longer exists, or because of poor performance.

An important power of the governor is to control the rate at which money is spent by the state. The General Assembly must approve a special bill before any money can be spent. The governor submits a pro-

POWERS OF THE GOVERNOR

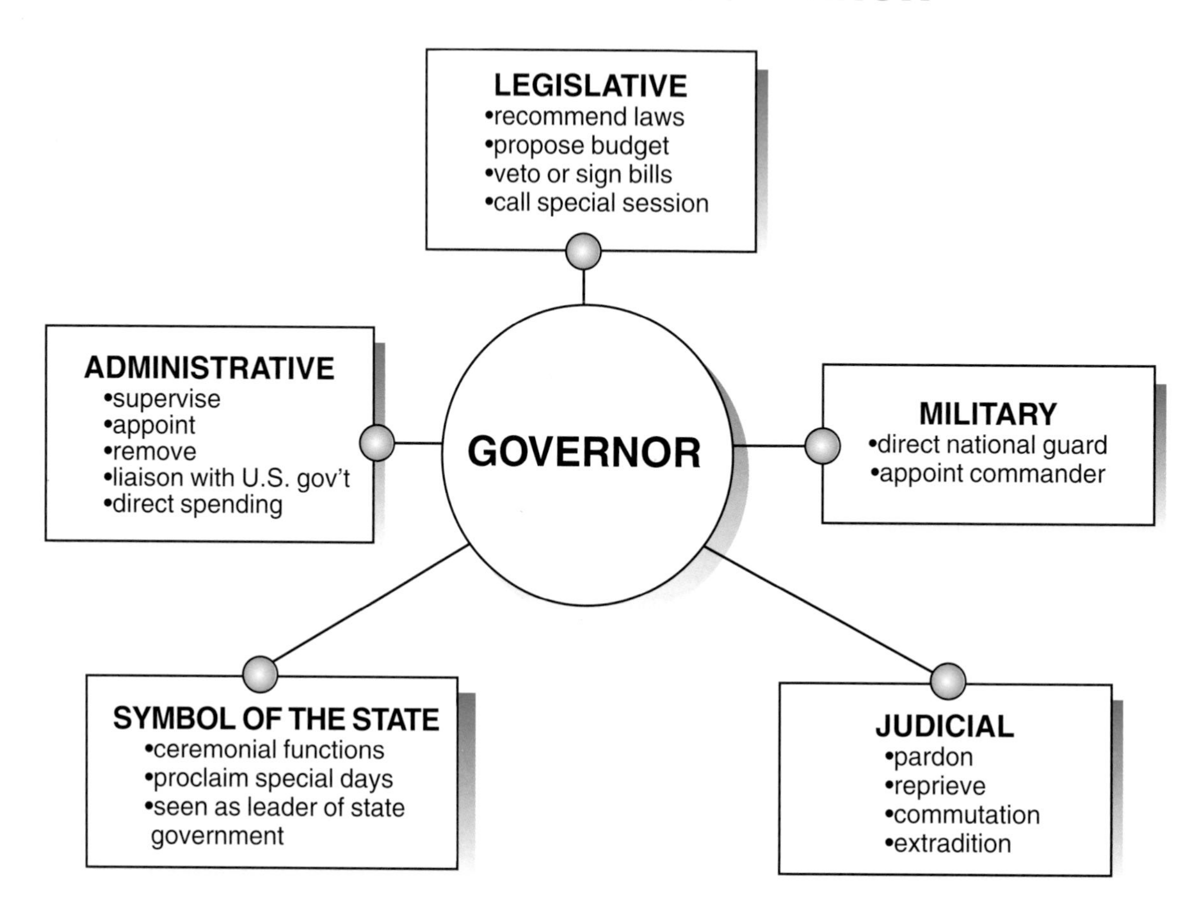

posed budget recommending various expenses, sometimes including tax increases. Unlike the federal budget which allows borrowing to pay for services, Missouri law requires that its budget be balanced every year.

After the bill is signed, the governor controls how fast money is spent or whether there should be cuts to prevent ***deficit spending.*** Deficit spending means spending more than the budget specifies.

The governor also has the job of providing ***liaison*** between the state and national governments. Liaison means "go between" or "contact person." Many national laws call upon the states to provide services, such as welfare and disaster relief, for which the federal government provides money. The governor is required to report back to the federal government how that money was used.

SECOND REGULAR SESSION

[TRULY AGREED TO AND FINALLY PASSED]

SENATE BILL NO. 643

83RD GENERAL ASSEMBLY

AN ACT

Authorizing the governor to convey certain state property located in Aurora, Missouri of this state in exchange for certain other property owned by Aurora, Missouri.

VETO

Be it enacted by the General Assembly of the State of Missouri, as follows:

Section 1. 1. The governor is hereby authorized and
2 empowered to grant, bargain and sell, convey and confirm
3 to the city of Aurora, Missouri, certain property located in
4 the city of Aurora, Missouri, which is currently being used
5 as an armory by the Missouri National Guard, in con-
6 sideration for property conveyed by the city of Aurora,
7 Missouri, to the state of Missouri by deed. The property to
8 be conveyed to the city of Aurora, Missouri, by the state of
9 Missouri is more particularly described as follows:
10 All that part of the Northeast Quarter (NE1/4) of the

The large stamp of a veto (meaning, "I forbid") looms across the front of a rejected senate bill.

Q:

HOW CAN EACH OF THE ADMINISTRATIVE POWERS BE USED TO CARRY OUT LAWS?

DISCUSSION: WHAT WOULD HAPPEN IF ALL OF THE JOBS IN THE EXECUTIVE BRANCH WERE UNDER THE MERIT SYSTEM?

2. ***Legislative Powers.*** In the last chapter we learned that the governor is part of the law-making process. He or she may recommend that new laws be made. The governor must propose a state ***budget*** in the first 30 days of each year's General Assembly session. This budget must include an estimate of ***revenue*** (income) to the state and a plan for spending it. Many important laws begin with the governor's office.

Almost all bills passed by the General Assembly are sent to the governor for approval. The governor must act on a bill within 15 days of receiving it. However, the governor has 45 days to act if the General Assembly ***adjourns,*** or ends the session, during this time. The governor can either sign or veto the bill. If it is signed, it becomes law after the waiting period. If the governor vetoes the bill, it is sent back to the house from which it came with an explanation for the veto. The General Assembly can override a veto by passing the law again with a two-thirds vote. Or an approved bill can become law if

Among the many responsibilities of Missouri's state highway officers is seeing that traffic flows smoothly, giving drivers safe passage. Here, an officer assists with a vehicle that has lost one of its hubcaps.

the governor takes no action at all, in which case the General Assembly passes a joint resolution telling the secretary of state to make the bill an "authentic act."

A bill to spend money is called an ***appropriation bill.*** The governor may veto one or more parts of such a bill and approve the rest. Bills to spend money for public schools and to pay state debts are exceptions to this power. The power to veto any part of a spending bill is called a ***line item veto.*** Most state governors have this power. While the Congress did adopt the line item veto, and the President signed it and used it, it was stricken by the Federal courts and will not be used again in its present form.

The governor may call a ***special session*** of the General Assembly to work on a particular issue that was not resolved during the regular session, such as taxes.

Q:

WHAT ACTIONS CAN THE GOVERNOR TAKE TO GET THE GENERAL ASSEMBLY TO PASS A LAW THAT HE OR SHE WANTS?

3. ***Military Powers.*** The governor is the commander-in-chief of the state ***national guard.*** The commander of the national guard, the adjutant-general, is appointed by the governor. The guard may be used for many purposes as decided by the governor.

In Missouri, the guard has been used to help towns wrecked by floods and tornados. The national guard could also be used to keep order during a riot, or to help enforce laws. The President of the United States may "nationalize" the armed forces. The governor loses authority over the guard if this happens.

There has recently been argument about who controls the national guard. The question is whether the governor may refuse to allow the guard to be used by the President in peacetime. The answer is "No"; the President controls the national guard.

DISCUSSION: WHY MUST THE GOVERNOR BE VERY CAREFUL ABOUT HOW THE NATIONAL GUARD IS USED?

SHOULD THE GOVERNOR BE ABLE TO REFUSE THE ORDERS OF THE PRESIDENT IN PEACETIME?

4. ***Judicial Powers.*** The governor has the power to act as a "final court." The governor may grant a pardon, reprieve, or commutation to a person convicted of a state crime. A ***pardon*** is complete release with "forgiveness"; it implies that a person admits guilt by accepting forgiveness. A ***reprieve*** postpones or delays a sentence, such as delaying an execution while new evidence is being sought. A ***commutation*** is reduction of a sentence given by a court.

   The governor also has power to grant extradition. Persons accused of a crime in one state may flee to another state in an attempt to avoid arrest. ***Extradition*** is a process used to return such a person to the state where the

The Great Seal was adopted in 1822 and contains many symbols:

- The grizzly bears represent strength and bravery.
- The Latin words mean "The welfare of the people is the supreme law."
- The new moon is a symbol of early Missouri's small size and wealth.
- The roman numerals are 1820, the year of statehood. The helmet represents sovereignty.
- The 23 stars are for the other states at the time Missouri joined the union.
- The U.S. coat of arms is for the national government.

Summary of Executive Branch Elected Officials

OFFICE	TERM	QUALIFICATIONS	BASIC POWERS
Governor	Four years (limited to two terms)	30 years old U.S. citizen 15 years Live in state 10 years	Administer laws Appoint/remove officials Liaison with federal gov't. Recommend laws & budget Sign or veto bills Call special session Command national guard Grant pardon, reprieve, or commutation Ceremonial head of state
Lieutenant Governor	Four years	30 years old U.S. citizen 15 years Live in state 10 years	Ex-officio President of the Senate Succeed to governorship Acting governor when needed Volunteer coordinator Ombudsman
Secretary of State	Four years	25 years old U.S. citizen Live in state one year	Non-financial record keeper Prepare ballots Certify elections
Attorney General	Four years	30 years old U.S. citizen Live in state one year	Chief legal officer Prosecute and defend state cases Give advisory opinions
Treasurer	Four years (limited to two terms)	U.S. citizen Live in state one year	Chief financial officer Care for and invest state funds
Auditor	Four years	30 years old U.S. citizen 15 years Live in state 10 years	Check collection and spending of money by state agencies Approve depositories Set up accounting system for state and local government

crime took place. Our governor may request that another state's governor send back a person accused of a crime in Missouri. However, the accused may remain in the new state if its governor refuses to grant extradition.

> **Q:**
>
> WHY IS THE GOVERNOR'S OFFICE SOMETIMES REFERRED TO AS A "FINAL COURT"?

5. ***Symbol of the State.*** The governor has another "power" that is not clearly defined in law. This power makes the governor the state leader, meaning that he or she may represent Missouri in meetings with groups from other countries. The governor may officially open a highway or bridge in a ribbon-cutting ceremony, or issue a proclamation to celebrate a special day. These events are called ***ceremonial*** functions. While they do not involve great power, they give the governor important media attention that will help make him more popular with the voters.

> **Q:**
>
> WHAT ARE SOME RECENT EXAMPLES OF THE GOVERNOR ACTING AS "SYMBOL OF THE STATE"?

LIEUTENANT GOVERNOR

The Missouri constitution makes the ***lieutenant governor*** the ex-officio president of the state Senate with the power to serve as governor if the elected governor leaves office. This may happen due to the death, resignation, disability, or impeachment of the governor. The lieutenant governor then serves until the end of the governor's term. The governor may take back the office after recovery, if absence is due to a disability.

The lieutenant governor also serves as acting governor when the governor is out of the state. The lieutenant governor is an ex-officio member of the Board of Public Buildings, and acts as state volunteer coordinator and ***ombudsman.*** An ombudsman is a person who investigates complaints by private citizens against government officials and agencies.

The lieutenant governor is elected for a four-year term at the same time that the governor is elected and may be reelected to this position. Unlike the governor there is no limit to the number of times the lieutenant governor can be reelected. The constitutional qualifications to fill the office of lieutenant governor are:

- at least 30 years of age
- U.S. citizen for at least 15 years
- resident of Missouri for at least 10 years

The same political qualifications apply to this job as to the job of governor. Candidates for governor and lieutenant governor from the same party may run as a team. However, voters choose the governor and lieutenant governor separately. This means that these two officers may be from different political parties.

SECRETARY OF STATE

The ***secretary of state*** is another top official in the executive branch. The person elected to this office serves a four-year term. There is no limit to the number of times this official may be reelected. Qualifications for this office are:

- at least 25 years old
- U.S. citizen
- resident of Missouri for at least one year

The secretary of state acts as the state's non-financial record keeper. This position has many different duties, which include:

- prepare ballots for state elections
- certify the results of state elections

- administer laws that require candidates to show where money for their campaigns came from
- register all Missouri corporations
- supervise the registration of all securities in the state, such as stocks and bonds
- place the state seal on official documents
- keep the official record of the governor's actions

ATTORNEY GENERAL

The ***attorney general*** is the chief legal officer of the state. This official is also elected to a four-year term, and there is not limit to the number of times this person may be reelected. Qualifications include:

- at least 30 years old
- a U.S. citizen
- a licensed attorney
- resident of Missouri for at least one year

The attorney general is responsible for prosecuting or defending all cases in which the state is involved. This official supervises lawyers who work for the attorney general's office and does not often personally appear in court.

The office of the attorney general is responsible for defending the state if it is sued. If someone were injured because of something done by a state worker while on the job, the state could be considered ***negligent***. To be negligent means to have helped cause an injury that should have been prevented. The injured person might sue the state in court for ***damages,*** meaning the amount of money the court would award because the state worker caused the injury.

Legal advice from this office is often requested by other state and local officials. Written advice is called an ***advisory opinion*** and is just that—an opinion. It is not law. A state officer or department almost always follows an advisory opinion.

STATE TREASURER

The state treasurer is the chief financial officer of the state and is elected to a four-year term, and, like the governor, is limited to two terms in office. The qualifications for this office are:

- U.S. citizen
- resident of Missouri for at least one year

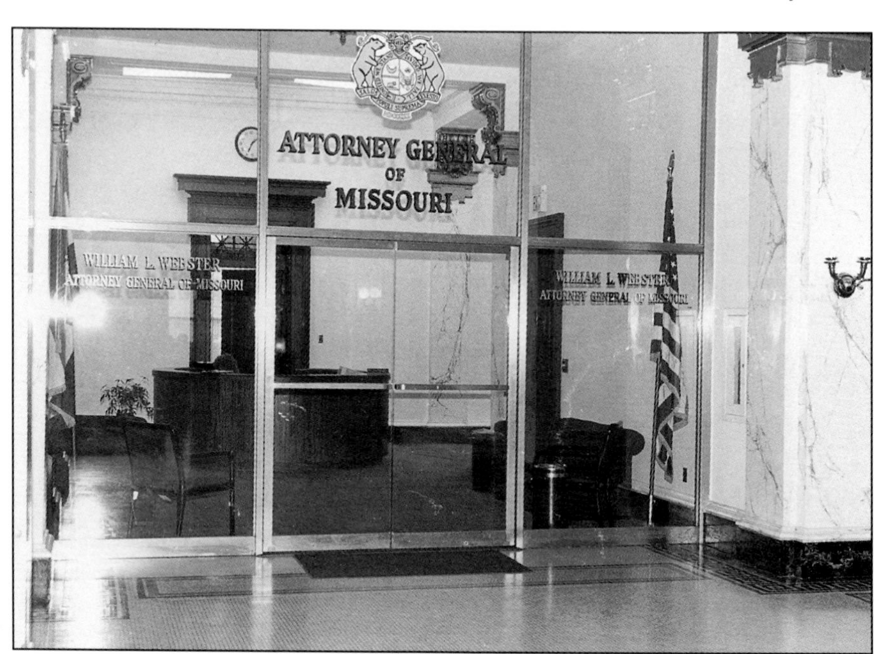

The large glass front of the Attorney General's office welcomes Missouri constituents to enter and air any grievances they may have that would involve legal action by this office.

The state treasurer takes care of all state funds and must determine the amount of money needed for current expenses of the state. The treasurer must safely invest all state income until it is spent. In this way, the state can earn income.

STATE AUDITOR

Qualifications for the office of ***state auditor*** are the same as for governor, serving the same four-year term. There is no limit to the number of times this person can be reelected

The auditor sets up the accounting system for the state and local government, and checks the collection and spending of money by all state officers and agencies. The auditor approves the places chosen by the treasurer to put state money. These places are called ***depositories.*** The purpose of this duty is to make sure that tax money will be safe.

BOARDS AND COMMISSIONS

There are more than 350 ***boards and commissions*** in the state. Each has certain powers. They make rules or recommend action on special subjects. Members are appointed for terms of 1 year to 4 or more years. Many members are appointed for political reasons. The boards and commissions are created by the General Assembly, or by the governor.

It is difficult to find many people willing to serve on boards or commissions, therefore many jobs have not been filled. Some of the things the commissions have recommended have not been done. This is often true if the General Assembly must approve money to be spent.

New boards and commissions are created as the General Assembly or the governor decide they are needed. Sometimes they are created to make rules about licensing people to do specific jobs, such as barbers, lawyers, and pharmacists.

Some examples of boards and commissions are:

- Jackson County Sports Complex Authority: regulates the sports facilities in the Kansas City area
- State Milk Board: enforces rules and inspections that concern fluid milk products
- Bi-State Development Agency: regulates public transportation in the St. Louis area in both Missouri and Illinois
- Governor's Committee on the Employment of the Handicapped: finds ways to create more jobs and training for handicapped people

DISCUSSION: SHOULD THE BOARDS AND COMMISSIONS BE ELIMINATED? IF YOU THINK SO, SHOULD THEIR JOBS BE GIVEN TO THE EXECUTIVE DEPARTMENTS UNDER THE GOVERNOR?

❐ SUMMARY

The executive branch carries out the laws made by the legislative branch. The governor also serves as a check on the power of the legislative branch. The executive branch is made up of several elected officials and many appointed ones. The result is that the power of the executive branch is greatly divided. The public is faced with a number of candidates running for different executive offices each election.

The governor is sometimes called the chief executive, having many powers to carry out laws and limit the General Assembly. Some of the major powers of the governor are appointment, removal, veto, and recommending laws. Others are acting as a final court for persons convicted of a crime, commanding the national guard, acting as liaison with the national government, and ceremonial functions.

There are several other leading executive officials who are elected. They are the lieutenant governor, secretary of state, attorney general, and state auditor. Each has a limited amount of power.

The executive branch also has more than 350 boards and commissions. Each may regulate or make recommendations about specific topics.

REVIEW

1. What is the purpose of the executive branch?
2. List the characteristics that a winning candidate for governor would likely have.
3. What happens if the governor dies or resigns from office?
4. How may the governor be removed from office?
5. List the major powers of the governor. Write a brief explanation beside each.
6. How may the governor serve as a check on the General Assembly?
7. What are the functions of the lieutenant governor?
8. List the other elected executive branch officials. Beside each write their major responsibilities.
9. What kinds of jobs are done by the boards and commissions in the Missouri executive branch?
10. Write a brief definition of each of the terms listed under "Terms to Look For" at the beginning of the chapter.
11. Putting together the information in this chapter and Chapter 2, how can the General Assembly check the power of the governor?

INVESTIGATE

Facts and Figures File:

Find out about each of the people who now hold the six major executive branch elected offices. Write a one-page article about each. You may need to use your local newspaper office or library to find back issues. You might also write to the office holder for information. Include the following:

- name
- political party
- how long in office
- other offices held
- size of vote in winning office, compared with opponent
- personal background (age, education, jobs held, family, etc.)
- political opinions
- well known groups and persons who support him or her
- things which he or she wants to accomplish while in office

PROJECT

An executive needs to have the ability to do a number of things in solving problems, such as:

- identify a problem
- find possible solutions
- consider limitations
- set a goal
- create a plan
- obtain the resources needed
- implement the plan (put it into effect)
- evaluate the plan
- make changes as needed

In this activity, you will become an executive. Your task is to identify a need in your school that is important to you and others. Write the problem and different possible solutions. Then list the limitations on your actions. Which of your solutions are now not possible? Choose what you think is the best of the remaining solutions. This becomes your goal.

Develop a step-by-step plan to reach your goal by listing the resources needed for your plan. These may include materials, people, and time. Putting dates on a calendar to do each step in your plan will help. You may have to change your plan when something unexpected happens. Remember to get the necessary permission in advance of doing each step of your plan.

Finally, put the plan into action—or, "implement" it. Look back on your plan when you are through. What parts were successful? What parts failed? What changes would you make if you were to do this again? Ask others to rate your ability to be an executive. Be sure to rate yourself.

POINT/COUNTERPOINT

This chapter mentions that there are some problems with having many elected executive officials and a lot of boards and commissions in our state. One possible alternative is to have an elected governor who appoints all the other top officials in the state. This is what the President of the United States can do in the national government.

Write a short essay that supports or opposes this idea. State as many reasons for your position as you can. Try to anticipate how someone would argue against your idea. Include points to counter what they would say.

Find people who agree with your point of view. They may give you more arguments on your side.

Have another student read your first draft and suggest changes. Rewrite your essay, checking for correct grammar and spelling. Your essay should have a title, introduction, body, and conclusion. Each paragraph should have a topic sentence.

In a bibliography at the end of your essay, list where you found the information and references that you used.

TERMS TO LOOK FOR

- federalism
- adversary system
- plaintiff
- defendant
- judicial review
- interpret
- precedent
- criminal case
- misdemeanor
- felony
- civil case
- tort
- liable
- constitutional law
- statutory law
- criminal law
- common law
- administrative law
- equity law
- injunction
- jurisdiction
- original jurisdiction
- appellate jurisdiction
- concurrent jurisdiction
- exclusive jurisdiction
- writ
- writ of habeas corpus
- transcript
- brief
- majority opinion
- concurring opinion
- dissenting opinion
- ordinance
- waive
- rebuttal
- unanimous
- Non-Partisan Court Plan
- hung jury
- commission
- Appellate Judicial Committee
- probable cause
- bond
- warrant
- circuit attorney
- arraignment
- information
- grand jury
- indictment
- preliminary hearing
- plea bargain
- verdict
- probation
- appeal
- case

4

The Judicial Branch

You have probably seen many news articles about courts. The court system makes up the judicial branch of government. Any of us may appear before courts. A person stopped for speeding in traffic may be brought before traffic court. If someone injures you, you may sue in court for damages. Courts determine the guilt of a person accused of a crime. There are two separate systems of courts in the United States. There are a number of courts that are part of the national government. Each state also has its own system of courts. This means that there are 50 state court systems and one national court system. These two separate court systems are an example of ***federalism*** in American government, meaning that the power is divided between the national and state governments. The judicial branch of the federal government serves as an umpire in disputes. These disputes may involve persons, companies, or governments. The constitution tries to create a balance between the three branches of government; the courts try to make

JUDICIAL SYSTEM

Look at the chart labeled "The Judicial System." Notice that the national court system deals with cases involving national laws, and the state courts deal with cases involving state laws. Both kinds of courts are limited by the United States Constitution. The state courts are limited by the state constitution, as well.

One purpose of the judicial system is to settle disputes between two parties. A dispute brought to a court is called a *case*; parties to a case may be people, companies, or the government.

There are always two sides in a case, and both sides want to win the dispute. This is called the ***adversary system.*** The side filing the complaint, or lawsuit, is called the ***plaintiff***; the side against which the complaint is filed is the ***defendant.***

Another purpose of the judicial system is to decide whether a law or action of government conflicts with the constitution. This is called ***judicial review.*** Judicial review requires that the courts ***interpret,*** or explain, the meaning of the constitution. A new interpretation of a part of the constitution will set a new ***precedent,*** or rule, to be followed in the future in similar cases.

Types of Cases

Courts handle two basic types of cases: criminal and civil. A ***criminal case*** involves an act that is in violation of the penal law and is an offense against the state or the United States.

Criminal cases are divided into misdemeanors and felonies. A ***misdemeanor*** is a lesser crime punished by less than a year in jail or less than a $1,000 fine. A ***felony*** is a major crime punishable by more than a year in jail or more than a $1,000 fine. The state is the plaintiff in a criminal case. The person accused of a crime is the defendant.

Generally, all cases not criminal in nature are classified as civil cases. In a ***civil case,*** an individual sues another for some reason. Sometimes the reason is that a person has broken a promise in a contract. Other times, a civil case can result from harm caused by the negligent act of another. A negligent act is committed when a person causes an injury to another by not exercising reasonable care in his or her actions. Often, the plaintiff wants damages in the form of money to compensate for the costs of the injury, such as medical expenses, lost wages, or pain and suffering. Divorces and bankruptcies are other examples of civil cases.

Negligence cases are just one example of what is called a ***tort:*** civil legal wrongs committed upon a person or property independent of contract. Other torts include product liability cases, civil assault, and libel and slander. In a tort action, the injured person becomes the plaintiff in the case. The person accused of causing the injury is the defendant Causing an accident is an example of a tort. The job of the court is to decide who is at fault and how much the damages should be. A person found at fault in a civil case is ***liable*** for damages. This means that they have to pay for the harm they caused.

A situation such as a car accident may involve both a criminal and a civil case. Suppose a driver runs into the back of another car while it is stopped for a red light. The act of hitting the other car is a misdemeanor crime and the driver who hit the other car would probably receive a traffic ticket from the police and have to go to court. If the court found the driver guilty, he or she would have to pay a penalty.

This accident would also involve a tort. The stopped car, and possibly its driver, would have been affected by the negligent act of the other driver. That driver could sue for damages for the harm done from the accident. For this reason, drivers need to have insurance to pay for damages if the court decides a driver is responsible for such a tort.

Courts apply different kinds of law in cases brought before them. The following are different kinds of law used in courts:

- ***Constitutional law*** involves past interpretations of the meaning of a part of the state or national constitution.

THE JUDICIAL SYSTEM

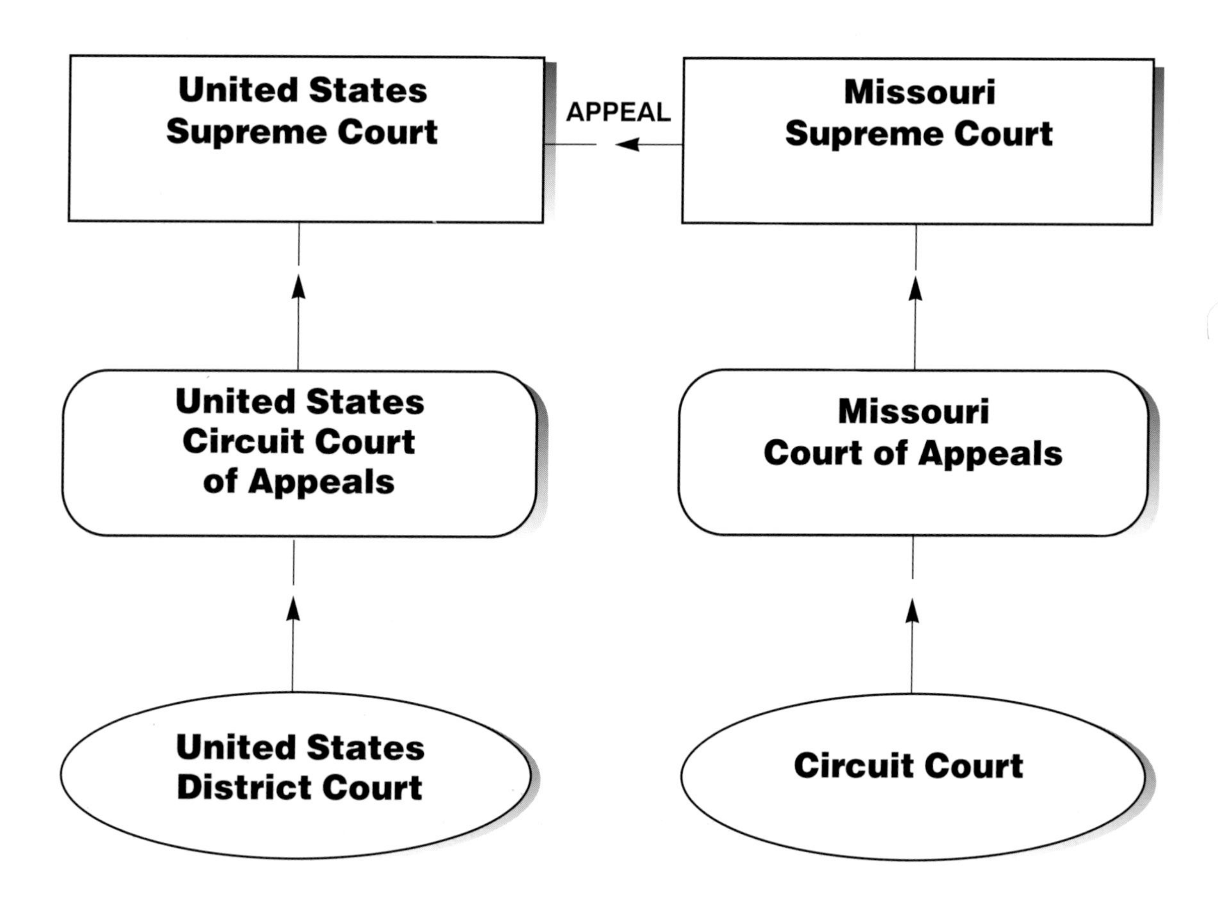

- *Statutory law* involves laws created by the legislative branch of government.
- *Criminal law* consists of statutes that make actions a crime.
- *Common law* is the decisions of courts made in past cases.
- *Administrative law* is a group of rules made by the executive branch of government.
- *Equity law* allows a person to go to court to prevent a harmful action. If the court agrees, it issues an ***injunction*** to stop the action. An injunction is a court order.

Jurisdiction of Courts

Each type of court has a ***jurisdiction.*** Jurisdictions means "the right to try a case." The kinds of cases a court may hear determine what kind of jurisdiction it has. There are several types of jurisdiction:

- *Original*—the first court to hear a case
- *Appellate*—a court that may review the decision of a lower court
- *Concurrent*—two courts may hear the same case
- *Exclusive*—only one court may hear the case

A court has original jurisdiction over a felony case if it is the first one to hear that case. A court that reviews the decision of the first court has appellate jurisdiction.

Q:

Why are there both federal and state courts?

What is a legal "case"?

What two jobs do the courts perform?

What is the difference between a civil and a criminal case?

What are the two kinds of criminal cases?

DISCUSSION: IN WHAT KINDS OF CASES WOULD EACH OF THE TYPES OF LAW BE USED?

RESEARCH: MAKE A LIST OF COMMON FELONIES AND MISDEMEANORS IN MISSOURI. GIVE AN EXAMPLE OF EACH FROM THE NEWSPAPER.

MISSOURI SUPREME COURT

The Supreme Court of Missouri is the highest court in the state. It is made up of seven judges. Every two years, the justices choose one of the members to be Chief Justice. The Chief Justice serves as chair of the court. Supreme Court judges serve a twelve-year terms.

The qualifications for the Supreme Court are that a person must be

- at least 30 years old.
- a U.S. citizen for at least 15 years.
- a qualified voter of Missouri for at least 9 years.
- licensed to practice law in Missouri.

One function of the Supreme Court is to hear appeals of cases that have been tried in a lower

Missouri's Supreme Court is in a three story, red brick French Renaissance-style building constructed in 1907. It stands opposite the capitol in Jefferson City and also houses the Attorney General's office. The building is well known for its massive marble staircase in the lobby and its two-story high library.

court. It may use the power of judicial review in making a ruling. This court also makes rules to be followed by other courts in the state.

Jurisdiction

The Supreme Court has several kinds of jurisdiction. It has appellate jurisdiction to hear cases on appeal from lower courts. The court has the power to decide whether it wishes to hear the appeal of most cases. If it refuses to hear a case, the last decision of a lower court stands. The court may order cases transferred to it from the Court of Appeals. This may happen in cases where the Court thinks the case is of general interest or importance. The Court may also believe that the law needs to be examined.

The Supreme Court has exclusive jurisdiction in some cases, such as those involving:

- whether a U.S. treaty or law is valid
- a part of the Missouri constitution
- who is entitled to hold a state office
- a death penalty having been imposed

The Supreme Court may issue orders called ***writs.*** One example is the ***writ of habeas corpus.*** This writ orders that a person being held be brought before a court. The purpose is to make sure that the person is not being illegally held.

The Supreme Court also has power to supervise all lower courts in the state. It creates the rules of procedure in these lower courts. When needed, it may also transfer court workers from one court to another for a short time. This could happen when one court has too many cases to handle.

Finally, the Court licenses all lawyers who practice in Missouri. It also may discipline any lawyer who violates the legal code of ethics.

Though it's now quiet and empty, this state Supreme Court chamber will serve as a court of last resort to hear arguments against decisions made earlier in a lower court.

Procedure

There is no trial when a case is argued before the Supreme Court. No witnesses appear and no evidence is introduced. An appeal is simply a review of what happened at the trial. The only evidence is a ***transcript*** of the trial. A transcript is a word-for-word recording.

The first step in an appeal to the Supreme Court is to prepare briefs. Each side in a case will file a ***brief,*** which consists of all the reasons why that side believes it is right. It will list many past precedents that agree with that side. The lawyers are saying, in effect, "The other judges in the past agreed with me. So should you."

The judges will schedule oral arguments for each side after they have read the briefs. At this time, the lawyers for each side will present their arguments to the Court. The judges may ask questions during the arguments. Then the judges meet in private conference to discuss both sides and make a decision. The decision is made by majority vote. This decision, and possibly the reasons for it, will be published. A decision may set a new precedent if it changes a rule that had been previously followed.

The written reasons of the majority of justices making a decision is called a ***majority opinion.*** A justice who agrees with the majority, but for a different reason, may write a ***concurring opinion.*** Justices who disagree with the decision may give their reasons in a ***dissenting opinion.*** These opinions may be signed or unsigned. Opinions give a guide to courts that will hear similar cases in the future.

Q:

What are the main functions of the Missouri Supreme Court?

How are decisions made by this court?

RESEARCH: REPORT ON A CASE RECENTLY IN THE NEWS WHICH HAS BEEN HEARD BY THE SUPREME COURT.

MISSOURI COURT OF APPEALS

The current Missouri Court of Appeals was created by a constitutional amendment in 1970. It consists of one Court of Appeals that has three districts. The Eastern District of the Court is located in St. Louis and has 14 judges. The Western District is in Kansas City and has 11 judges. The Southern District meets in Springfield or Poplar Bluff and has seven judges. Each district court may choose to create divisions of its court. The eastern and western districts have done this.

There are 32 judges on the Court of Appeals. The qualifications to be a members of this court are the same as for the Supreme Court. Members may serve a term of 12 years.

Jurisdiction

The Court of Appeals has appellate jurisdiction in all cases that are not in the exclusive jurisdiction of the Supreme Court. Remember that the Supreme Court may also transfer a case to itself if it believes that an important issue is at stake. The Court of Appeals may also issue writs, but the main function of this court is to determine whether any error took place in the lower court. It is a chance to review what happened in a trial. Most appeals end with the Court of Appeals.

Procedure

An appeal is heard by a group of judges. They may be the judges of the entire district or a division of the district. Briefs are filed and oral arguments are made before the judges, but no new evidence is brought in and no witnesses are heard. A decision is made by a majority vote of the judges. The court may affirm the lower court's decision. This means

Typical Courtroom Setting

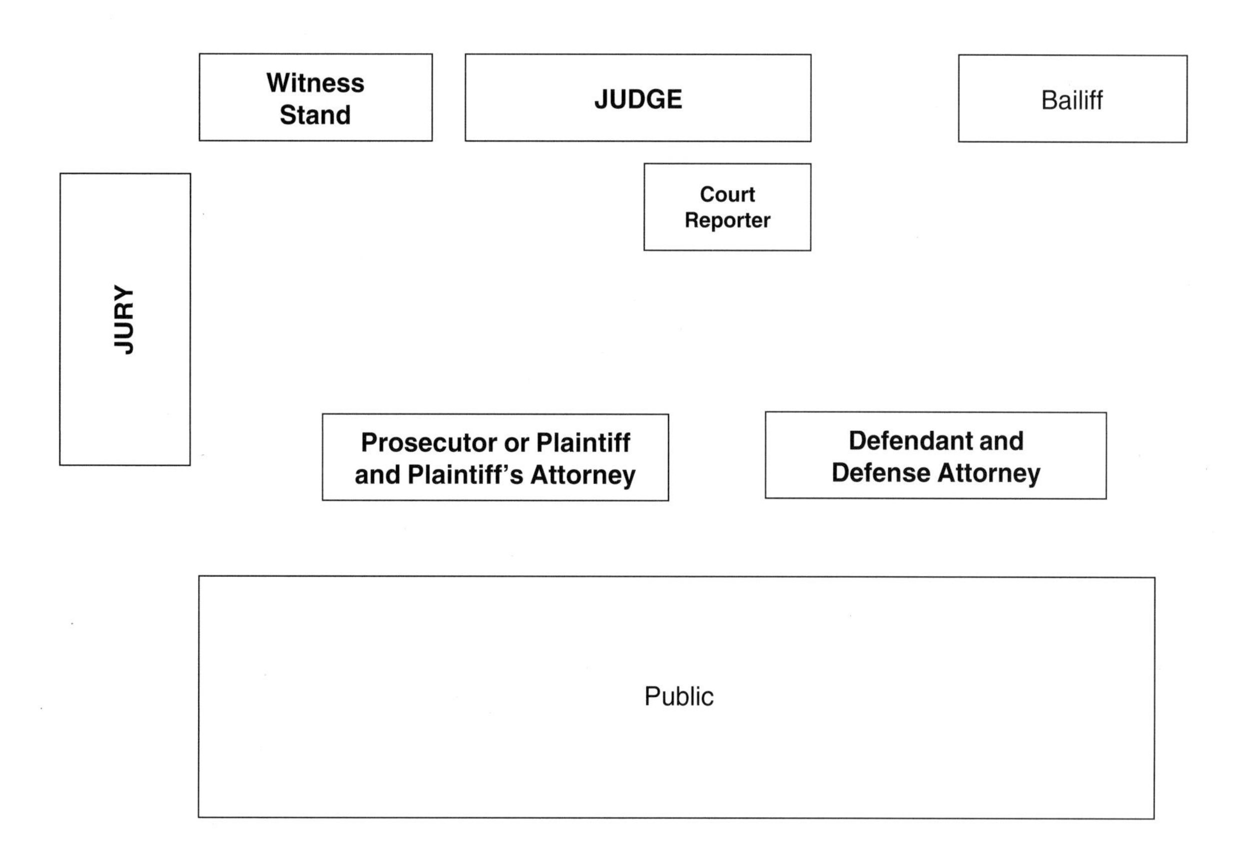

that no change is made in that decision. The court may also overturn the lower court decision. If this happens, there may be a new trial or the accused may be released.

Q:

How is the Court of Appeals different from the Supreme Court? How is it similar?

MISSOURI CIRCUIT COURTS

All trials begin in Circuit Court. There are 45 judicial circuits within the state. The number of circuit judges is set by the General Assembly. The constitution requires a minimum of one judge in each circuit.

There are three levels within the circuit courts: the circuit division, the associate circuit division, and the municipal division. Each circuit judge appoints a court reporter to take transcripts. Each circuit court also appoints a juvenile officer. Each county chooses a circuit clerk.

There is at least one associate circuit judge in each county. The state may approve more such judges depending on a county's population. Communities with more than 400,000 people must set up a municipal division with a municipal judge to preside. Smaller communities may do the same or ask that the associate division hear local cases. Municipal judges are paid by local communities. Other circuit judges are paid by the state.

Judges of the Circuit Court serve a six-year term. Municipal division judges have a term set by their communities. It is often four years. The qualifications of circuit judges are:

- at least 30 years of age
- resident of the circuit that they serve
- a U.S. citizen for at least 10 years
- a qualified voter in Missouri for at least 3 years
- licensed to practice law in Missouri

Jurisdiction

Circuit courts are the courts of original jurisdiction for civil and criminal cases. They are the first courts to hear a case. Trials with witnesses and evidence presented take place at this level. Judges of the municipal division hear cases involving local ***ordinances.*** Ordinances are laws made by the local government. Cases involving ordinances in communities that have no municipal division may be heard in the associate division.

Procedure

A trial will be held in Circuit Court if a person is accused of a crime and pleads "not guilty." The accused has the right to a jury trial. He or she may ***waive*** (give up) this right. The case is then heard only by the judge. Trials involving civil lawsuits are also heard in Circuit Court.

A trial is heard by 12 jurors and one alternate, if a jury is used. Evidence is presented and witnesses are heard. Both sides may present their case. Each side may also try to argue against what the other side has presented. This is called ***rebuttal*** argument. If there is a jury, the judge give instructions to it regarding the law. The jury then discusses the case and votes. In order to decide the outcome of a criminal case, all jurors must agree on a single decision. This is called a ***unanimous*** vote. Such a vote will find the accused either guilty or innocent. If the jury cannot reach a unanimous decision, it is called a ***"hung jury"*** and another trial will have to take place or the accused released. A vote of three-fourths of the jurors is needed to decide a civil case.

Q:

What kinds of cases are heard in Circuit Court?

When does a decision of the jury have to be unanimous?

What is the major difference between Circuit Court and the higher courts?

HOW JUDGES ARE CHOSEN

A large number of judges in Missouri are chosen by what is called the ***Non-Partisan Court Plan.*** It has become known nationally as the Missouri Plan or Merit Selection. This way of choosing judges has been copied by many states.

The plan is applied to a number of different courts in Missouri:

- Missouri Supreme Court
- Missouri Court of Appeals
- Circuit or Associate Circuit judge in Jackson County and the city of St. Louis
- Circuit or Associate Circuit judges in any

OFFICIAL
JUDICIAL BALLOT
STATE OF MISSOURI
TUESDAY, NOVEMBER 4, 1986
Submitting to the voters whether the Judges named below, whose terms expire December 31, 1986, shall be retained in their offices for new terms.
VOTE ON EACH JUDGE.

SUPREME COURT JUDGE

Shall Judge EDWARD D. ROBERTSON of the Supreme Court of the State of Missouri be retained in office?

YES ☐ NO ☐
(Mark an X in the box you prefer)

MISSOURI COURT OF APPEALS JUDGES EASTERN DISTRICT

Shall Judge GERALD M. SMITH of the Eastern District Court of Appeals be retained in office?

YES ☐ NO ☐
(Mark an X in the box you prefer)

Shall Judge GARY M. GAERTNER of the Eastern District Court of Appeals be retained in office?

YES ☐ NO ☐
(Mark an X in the box you prefer)

Shall Judge JOHN J. KELLY, JR. of the Eastern District Court of Appeals be retained in office?

YES ☐ NO ☐
(Mark an X in the box you prefer)

Sample Ballot

other circuits, if approved by a vote of the people. The plan may be ended in these circuits by a vote of the people. Judges are directly elected in circuits where the plan is not used.

The plan combines appointment with a kind of election. A special ***commission*** is created to nominate three qualified persons for a judgeship. There is one commission to nominate judges for the Supreme Court or any court of appeals. It is called the ***Appellate Judicial Commission.*** It is made up of a Supreme Court judge, a person chosen by the lawyers in the state, and another person appointed by the governor. This person must come from the people who live in the court of appeals district. The members of the commission choose their chairman.

Another commission is created for each circuit to nominate judges for circuit court. Each of these commissions has five members. One is the judge who is president of the district court of appeals in that circuit. Lawyers in the circuit choose two more members. The governor also chooses two non-lawyers who live in the circuit.

The Supreme Court sets the term of members of each commission. It also makes rules for them. Decisions of commissions are made by majority vote. Members receive no pay except for expenses.

A commission nominates three qualified persons when a judgeship position opens. The governor then must appoint one of the three within sixty days. The commission makes the choice if the governor does not do so. The person appointed then serves his or her term; for example, the term of members of the Court of Appeals is 12 years. At the end of the term, a judge may ask for another term by writing to the secretary of state. If the judge does this, the people have the opportunity to vote at a general election whether to keep him or her.

No political party is shown on the ballot. The ballot reads:

SHALL JUDGE (name of judge) OF THE (name of court) COURT BE RETAINED IN OFFICE? ☐Yes ☐No

The judge begins to serve another term if a majority of those voting on the question vote "yes." If a majority votes "no," the commission recommends three other people. The governor than appoints one of the three to fill the job.

There is yet another commission called the Commission on Retirement and Discipline. This commission may recommend to the Supreme Court that a judge be removed, retired, or disciplined. The Supreme Court may then choose to take one of those actions. In this way a judge may be removed during his or her term.

DISCUSSION: WHAT ARE THE ADVANTAGES AND DISADVANTAGES OF THE NON-PARTISAN COURT PLAN? WOULD APPOINTMENT BY THE GOVERNOR OR DIRECT ELECTION BE BETTER OR WORSE?

STEPS IN A FELONY CASE

A felony criminal case goes through many stages. It starts with arrest and ends with an acquittal or a chance for appeal. The constitution requires that the rights of the accused be protected at all times. The following are typical steps in a felony case:

1. The alleged act
   A felony has been committed.
2. The arrest
   The police arrest a person they have "probable cause" to believe committed the crime. ***Probable cause*** exists if the evidence leads the police to believe that the person probably committed the crime. The accused is brought to a police station for "booking" and processing. The accused is assigned an arrest number, and is then photographed and fingerprinted. It is determined if there is a previous arrest record. Police prepare a report of the crime and arrest. The accused may be locked up at police headquarters or may be released on bond at this time. ***Bond*** is an amount of money which the accused deposits to guarantee his or her return for trial. A person released on bond is given a date for preliminary hearing.
3. Application for warrant
   The arresting police officer presents the charges against the accused to the Circuit Attorney. The Circuit Attorney prosecutes criminal cases in the circuit. This official decides whether to prosecute the accused. The victim, witnesses, and other evidence may be present. The accused is not present. Probable cause for the arrest is shown. The accused must be released if a warrant is not obtained within 20 hours of arrest. The ***warrant*** lists the charges made against the accused. The ***circuit attorney*** may change the charges if desired.
4. Associate Circuit Court ***arraignment*** hearing
   This is a hearing for a person not on bond. The accused is told of the charges, the date of the preliminary hearing, and the amount of bond needed.
5. Filing of charges
   The circuit attorney may file ***information*** with the clerk of the circuit court. It states that the attorney intends to go to trial on certain charges. The Circuit Attorney may choose to attempt to get a grand jury indictment instead. A ***grand jury*** is a group of 12 people who hear evidence to see if a person should be charged with a crime. It is not a trial of the accused. The grand jury may vote a "true bill" of indictment if they agree that there is enough evidence to go to trial. An ***indictment*** charges a person with a crime. Grand juries are called by the presiding judge of the circuit. Most cases go to trial through information.
6. Preliminary hearing in Associate Circuit Court
   A ***preliminary hearing*** is used if the prosecutor brings charges through information. A judge hears evidence presented by the prosecutor, victim, accused, witnesses, and arresting officer. The judge decides whether there is enough evidence for a trial. This does not mean the accused is guilty. The hearing prevents a person from being brought to trial on too little evidence. The case is dropped if the judge finds there is not enough evidence.

7. Bonding decision
   This event takes place after either the preliminary hearing or a grand jury decides that the accused will go to trial. The judge must decide whether the accused may continue to be out of jail on bond. The conditions of the bond may be changed. Remember that the purpose of a bond is to guarantee that the accused will return for trial. The bond may be in the form of money or another kind of guarantee. The accused is sent to jail if there is no bond allowed or the accused does not provide the money for it.

8. Arraignment hearing in the Circuit Court
   Here the accused is formally told of the charges for which he or she will be tried. The accused then enters a plea to the charge. The plea may be "guilty as charged" or "innocent." The accused may also agree to plead guilty to a lesser charge. This is sometimes called a ***plea bargain.*** The accused may receive a lesser penalty and the state does not have to go to trial. The court may also order a mental examination of the accused if it appears to be needed. A special hearing may be held for this purpose. A date for sentencing is set if the accused has pleaded guilty.

Steps in a Felony Case

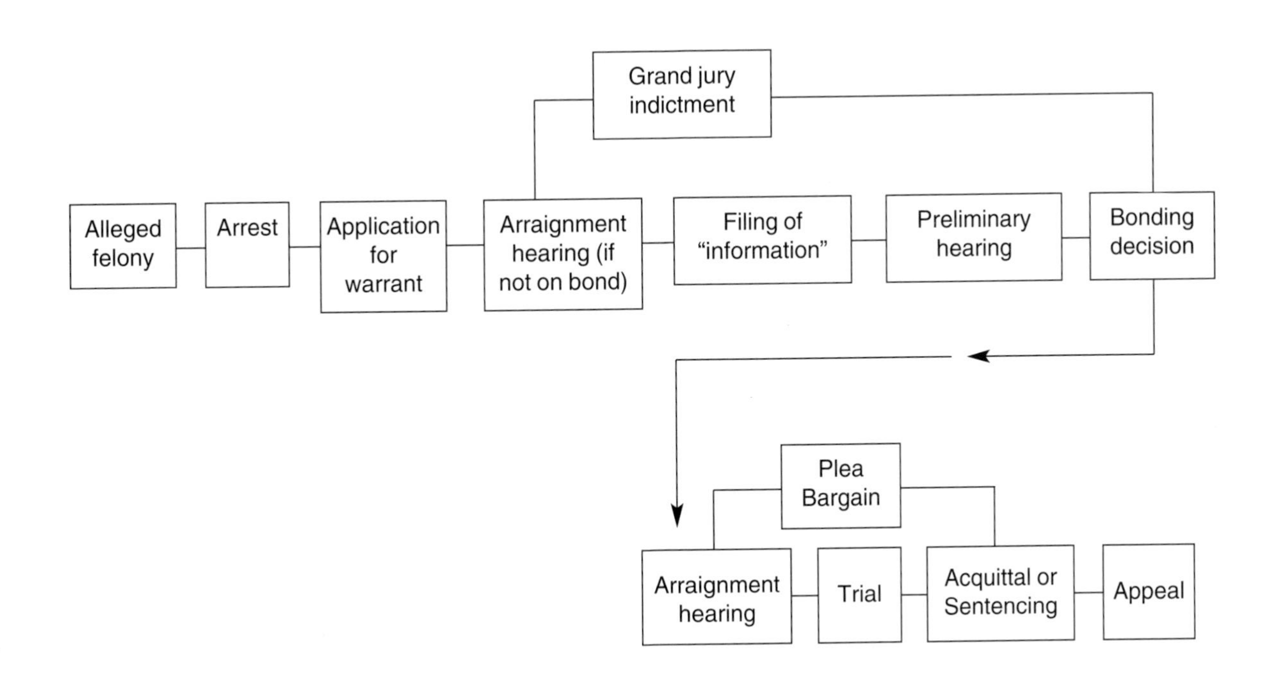

9. Trial
   The next step for a person who has pleaded innocent is trial. Here the case is heard by a jury. The accused may also ask to have the case heard by a judge only. Witnesses for both sides give testimony, and evidence is shown. Attorneys for both sides give arguments. Finally, a jury or the judge makes a decision. This decision is called a ***verdict.*** The accused is released if the jury or judge finds him or her innocent. If the verdict is guilty, a sentencing date is set. In some cases the jury is not able to reach a unanimous decision. When this happens, a new trial may be ordered or the case may be dropped.
10. Sentencing
   The judge will likely request a pre-sentencing investigation of the accused's past. The person's spouse, employer, friends, and others may be asked for information. The judge will then pronounce sentence. The penalty for a crime is provided in the law. The judge may have some choice as to how severe to make the sentence. A judge may grant ***probation*** instead of a sentence in some cases. Probation requires that the accused follow certain rules and report to a parole office instead of going to prison.
11. Appeal
   A person convicted of a crime may choose to ***appeal*** a guilty verdict. This means they are asking the Court of Appeals to review the case. The Court of Appeals may decide that there was nothing wrong with what happened at the trial. It may also decide that the rights of the accused may have been violated. The judge may have made a mistake. The Court may order a new trial or the release of the accused if there was a problem with the first trial.

What is the purpose of each of the steps in a felony case?

At what steps in the process can the accused be released?

DISCUSSION: MANY STEPS IN THE PROCESS ARE PROVIDED TO PROTECT THE ACCUSED. ARE THERE ENOUGH OF THESE PROTECTIONS? TOO MANY? SHOULD PLEA BARGAINS BE ALLOWED?

❒ SUMMARY

The Missouri judicial system is separate from the federal judicial system. It is made up of three different types of courts. These are the State Supreme Court, Court of Appeals, and Circuit Courts. The purposes of these courts are to settle disputes and to interpret the meaning of law.

Both civil and criminal cases are heard by these courts. Circuit Courts have original jurisdiction. They are the courts where trials take place. The Court of Appeals and Supreme Court have mainly appellate jurisdiction. They review what happened in lower courts. Appellate courts do not hold trials; they examine transcripts of lower court trials and decisions.

Judges of the appellate courts and some circuit courts are chosen by the Non-Partisan Court Plan. This plan provides for a commission to nominate three persons to fill each judgeship. The governor then appoints one of the three to the job. The people may vote on whether to keep the judge at the end of his or her term. Other circuit judges are chosen by direct election.

Court cases go through a series of steps. These steps are designed to protect the rights of the accused and to convict the guilty. Many chances are provided to drop a case if there is not enough probable cause to continue. The system always assumes that the accused is innocent until proven guilty. The prosecution must provide proof that the accused is guilty.

REVIEW

1. Write a brief definition in your own words of the terms listed under "Terms to Look For" at the beginning of the chapter.
2. Explain why the judicial system in the United States is an example of the principle of federalism.
3. How is a tort different from a crime?
4. Give an example of a criminal and a civil case.
5. Make a chart with the headings shown below. Then fill in each of the columns for the three types of courts in Missouri:
   - Court
   - Qualifications
   - Term
   - Jurisdiction
6. Describe the basic jobs done by each of the three types of courts in Missouri.
7. Make a chart that shows the steps in a trial.
8. Suppose one of the Court of Appeals judges decided to retire during his or her term. List the steps that would have to take place to fill the vacancy.
9. How are the governor and the secretary of state involved in the Non-Partisan Court Plan for selection of judges?
10. Copy the chart in this chapter that shows the steps in a felony case. Below each heading, fill in what happens at that step.

INVESTIGATE

Facts and Figures File:

- List the name(s) of the Circuit Judge(s) and Associate Circuit Judges in your circuit. Where are their courts located?
- Find out how the idea of plea bargaining is used in your circuit. Try to interview a judge, attorney, or other court worker about this subject.
- Visit a court when a trial is in session. Make a log of what you see happening and report to your class.
- Make a list of people other than the judge who work at the court, such as the bailiff and court reporter. Describe what each does.
- Talk to a judge about the Non-Partisan Court Plan of selecting judges. Does he or she think it is a good idea? Why?
- Identify the rights of juveniles who are brought to court in Missouri.

PROJECT

In this project your class will act out the steps in a felony case. You will need someone to play the following roles:

- the accused
- arresting officer
- circuit attorney
- associate circuit judge
- defense attorney
- court clerk
- bailiff
- jurors
- witnesses
- friend of the accused

Simulate a theft, such as from a cabinet in the classroom. Be sure that the jurors do not see the alleged crime take place. Then follow each of the steps in the felony case described in this chapter. Your class may want to take a short time each day to do one of the steps in the process.

POINT/COUNTERPOINT

Some people feel that our judicial system protects the rights of the accused but not those of the victim. The victim often must

- pay for medical bills and repair to damaged property.
- give information to police but not be informed of progress in the investigation.
- provide his or her own transportation to police headquarters, prosecutor's office, and to court.
- miss work.
- relive the crime in front of the court.
- be subject to cross-examination.
- have the case presented by a prosecutor who works for the public, not the individual victim.
- accept having no right to object to a plea bargain.
- continue to live in fear of retaliation from the criminal.

Prepare a debate on this subject. One side will argue that the legal system must be the way it is in order to protect the rights of the accused against unreasonable government action. The other side will argue that changes are needed to protect the rights of the victim.

At the end of the debate, each member of the class should write an essay taking a stand on this issue.

TERMS TO LOOK FOR

- local government
- counties
- creatures of the state
- county charter
- decentralized
- home rule
- municipality
- incorporate
- city charter
- city council
- mayor
- weak mayor-council
- strong mayor-council
- board of aldermen
- board of trustees
- city administrator form
- city manager form
- city council form
- commission form
- school districts
- governing board

5

Local Government

If you think about the place where you live, you will see the everyday effects of local government around you. There are many different local governments. A ***local government*** is one that covers an area smaller than the entire state. You probably live in several of them at the same time. Counties, cities, villages, and special districts are some forms of local government. Local government laws permit and encourage communities and rural areas to have local laws that best fit their own needs. This results in different rules for different places. Local governments may make laws about such things as traffic lights, kinds of buildings allowed, types of classes in schools, and property taxes. They also provide many services such as education, water, sewers, road maintenance, and garbage disposal.

COUNTIES

All transportation was by horse in the early days of our state. This meant that going to the state capitol was a long and difficult trip. ***Counties*** were created to serve as agents of the state in each local area. They were made small so that people could do business with the government and return home in one day. Missouri now has 114 counties, plus the city-county of St. Louis. The constitution allows counties to divide or join together if half of the voters living in them approve.

Counties are often called ***creatures of the state.*** This is because they are created by the state government. Counties enforce many laws of the state. The state constitution and state laws set many rules about counties. They list the jobs that must be done by counties. The counties provide many different services to people who live in the county. Some of these county-wide services may include law enforcement, parks, road construction and maintenance, building inspections, health services, and jails. They also provide local services for people who do not live in cities or towns.

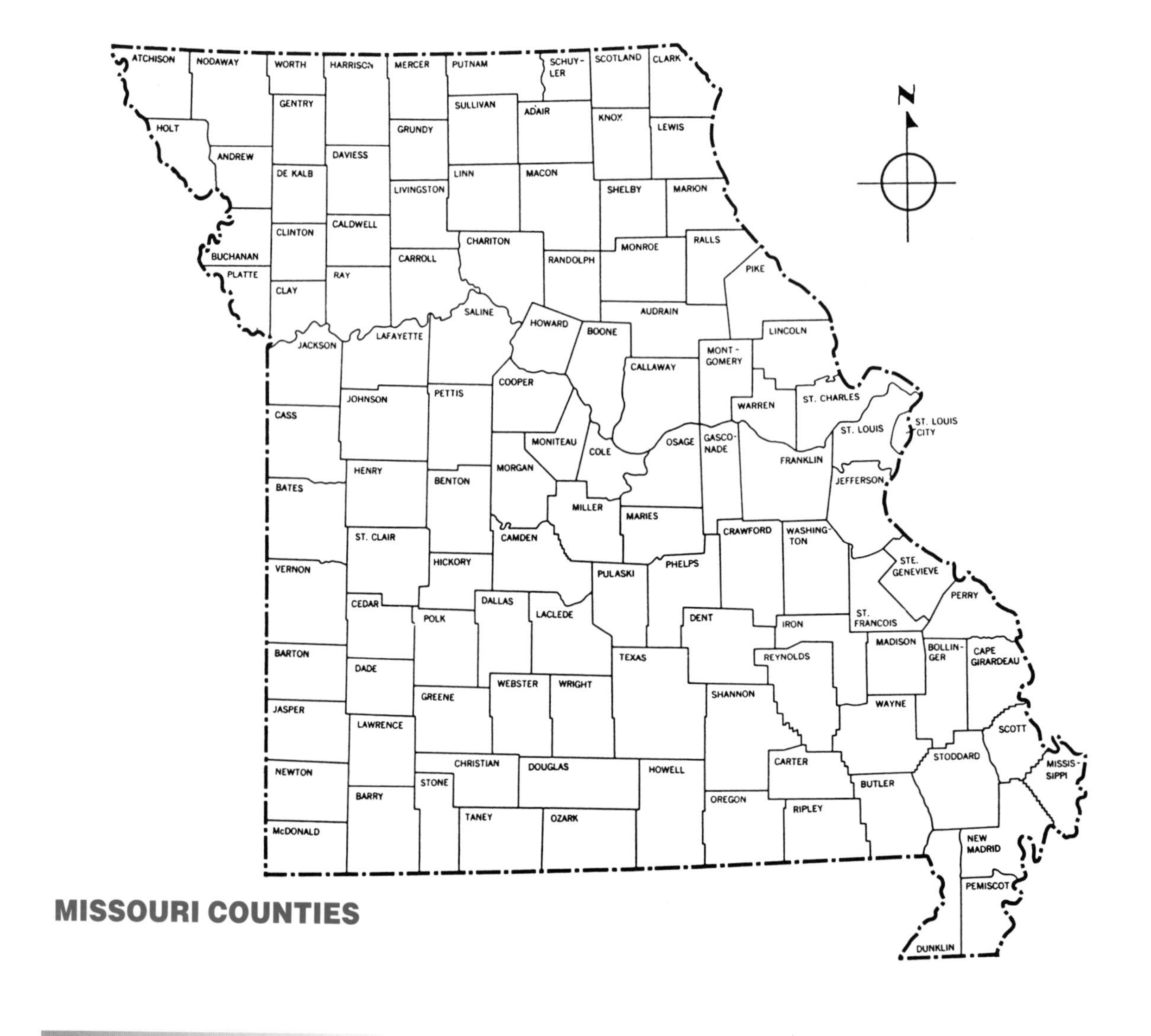

MISSOURI COUNTIES

Charter Counties

A county with more than 85,000 people may create a charter to set up its own government. A ***county charter*** is like a constitution for the county. The charter may not violate the rules set up by the state constitution. A county charter may include such things as

- how the county government is organized.
- how laws shall be made about county services outside of cities.
- what officers the county will have, and their duties.
- term of office and pay of county officers.
- powers and services of any city or town in the county.
- how the charter may be changed.

The people living in any community in the county have a chance to vote to accept or refuse limits set for them by the county. The people also have a chance to vote on how to pay for any of the jobs the county wants the community to do. All of this means that one county's government may look different from that of another county.

County road maintenance is an ongoing project, requiring pothole repairs, resurfacing and, often, widening.

County Commissions

All Missourians except residents of the City of St. Louis are under the jurisdiction of county government. County governments are important because of the services they are required to perform on behalf of the state.

For example, if a couple wants to get married, they get a marriage license from the office of the County Recorder of Deeds. If a citizen wants a hand gun permit, he or she must apply for it in the county sheriff's office. If a resident wishes to buy property, he or she can check ownership with the office of the county Recorder of Deeds and then have the purchase recorded. These are just a few of the services of county governments.

Notice that they do not include services such as fire protection. Such services are performed by municipalities or special districts.

Two of the more familiar county services are administering elections, and building and maintaining roads and bridges that lie outside of cities and villages.

The major decision-making body for most county governments is the County Commission. The commission is an administrative body consisting of a presiding commissioner elected from the entire county and two associate commissioners elected from districts. Each district has approximately half of the county's population.

Although county commissions administer most of the county business, they have little legislative authority. The Missouri General Assembly is, in effect, the county legislative body in all but the charter counties of St. Louis, Jackson, and St. Charles. Citizens of these three counties have approved adoption of charters, or mini-constitutions,

City parks offer a soft contrast to the sharp angles of the Kansas City skyline.The cities also maintain these parks, providing pleasant recreational facilities for entire families: from swing sets to baseball diamonds, and surfaced paths for bikers, roller bladers, and baby carriages.

that provide for legislative authority. Such authority involves the ability to pass local ordinances or laws, but they must not conflict with state law.

The county commission's most important function is budgetary. County budgets must be approved by the commission, as well as proposed changes in property and sales tax rates, which must be approved by a vote of the people. Budgeting is complicated and often controversial. State-mandated services and limited revenues have put many counties in financial jeopardy.

Although the county commission has budgetary authority and is the only body that can make decisions on behalf of the entire county, there are other important officials. The county clerk, treasurer, collector, and assessor have important responsibilities and each is elected at-large. This gives them some independence from the county commission, which is why county government is often called ***decentralized.*** It is an older and more traditional form of government than others.

Home Rule Counties

The so-called ***home rule*** counties have charters, or mini-constitutions approved by voters. They not only have legislative authority as noted, but are organized differently from the rest. This includes the concept of separation of powers, with the legislature being entirely separate from the executive branch.

The elected chief executive has more authority than a presiding commissioner and can appoint some officials, usually with council approval. The chief executive also has veto authority in some instances.

Each home rule county has a council similar to a city council, with members elected from districts. These councils pass ordinances, or local laws, and resolutions. This means that home rule counties can provide many urban services if they desire.

St. Louis County

St. Louis County is unlike other counties. It is the most urban of the metropolitan home rule counties. It not only has the most municipalities within its border, but acts as a municipality of last resort to its population outside of the cities. With its increased legislative authority through its charter and many special state laws, St. Louis County provides a variety of urban services to rural areas. Existing cities also like to provide such services through contracts because it results in greater revenues. Competition between the county and municipalities has existed for decades. The county fears the day most of its land is municipal, for it will lose much of its influence.

Q:

Why are counties called "creatures of the state"?

What are the limits set on county government?

What is the purpose of a county charter?

MUNICIPAL GOVERNMENT

Most of the people in Missouri live in a ***municipality.*** Municipalities vary widely in size from small villages to large cities. They are simply a local government organization serving the people who live together in a community.

There are several classes of municipalities in Missouri: 3rd class, 4th class, villages, constitutional charter cities, special charter cities, and more. Although the state constitution says there should be no more than four classes, this requirement has long been ignored. Constitutional charter cities adopt their own mini-constitutions by a vote of the people, as stated in the state constitution. Before 1875, a special charter city got its charter from the legislature in the form of a state law.

The class of a municipality depends of the number of people who live there when it is formed. If a city grows large enough to enter another class, there is no requirement that it change, as is the case with counties. If it does wish to change, voter approval is needed. This is the reason there are no 1st class or 2nd class cities; eligible cities chose to remain 3rd class cities, or they adopted charters. As a consequence, these statutes remained unused and were repealed, or cancelled, in 1975. More than half of Missouri's people live in cities, which are often termed "urban areas."

Municipalities are given certain powers to act as governments by the state laws and constitution. There are also limits set on the powers of municipalities. If people in a community wish to form a municipal government, they must first ***incorporate.*** This is done by a vote of the people in the community. If approved, election results are forwarded to the secretary of state, and the community becomes a legal entity with the power to tax.

Any municipality with more than 5,000 people may adopt a ***city charter.*** The process of charter drafting and adoption is known as "home rule." Missouri was the first state to authorize it by constitution in 1875. It allows flexibility in organizing city government, but is limited by state law. Another advantage is that the charter can be amended by a local vote. In non-charter cities, if an amendment is desired, the General Assembly has to change the appropriate state law, which then changes it for every other city in the same class.

A charter is written by a commission whose members are elected when voters approve the charter proposal. The commission has one year to develop a draft of its proposal, which then must be approved by voters. Most of Missouri's larger cities have adopted charters, but many cities that are eligible have not. Many citizens still prefer the

WEAK MAYOR-COUNCIL FORM

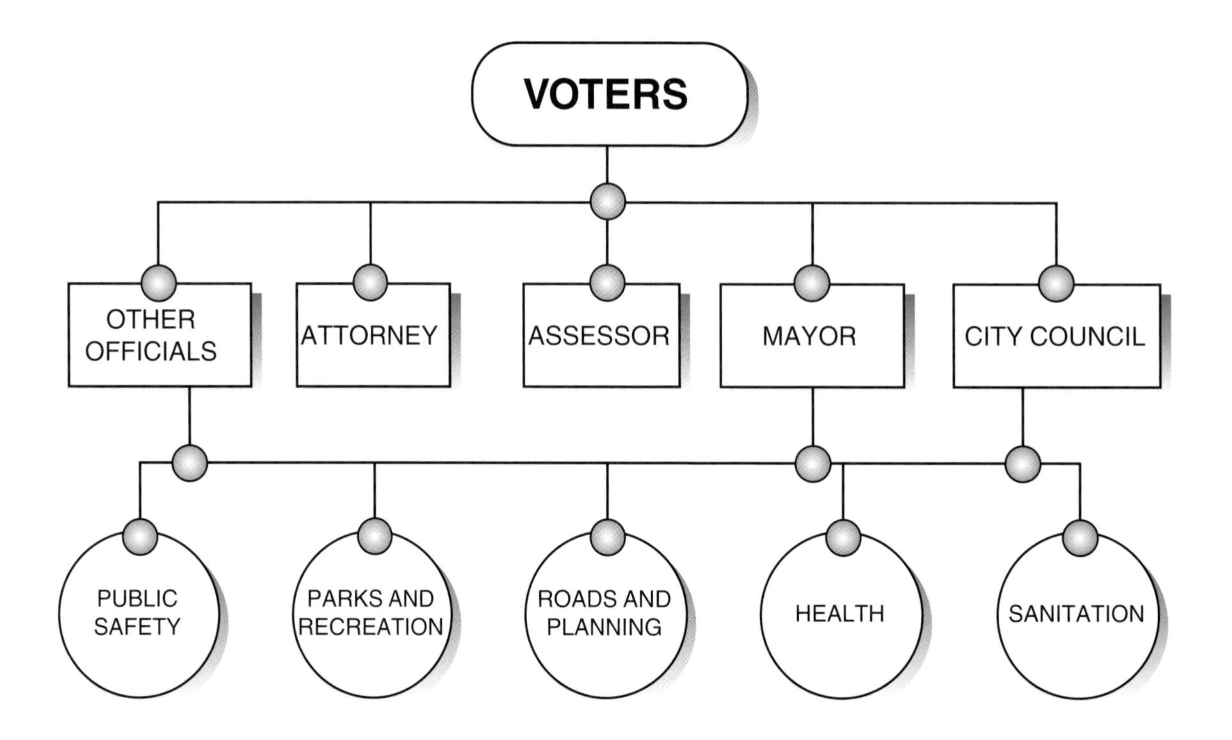

traditional, decentralized organizations they presently have and do not want to risk the charter process.

Forms of Municipal Government

There are several different forms of municipal government. Most are provided as packages by state law for one or more classes of cities. For example, cities of the 3rd class can adopt as a package the following forms:

- weak mayor-council
- stong mayor-council
- weak mayor-council-administrator
- commission
- city manager

Generally, only the weak mayor-council form is available to 4th class cities, but the strong mayor-council form is available only through charter drafting in home rule cities. Each form has some kind of legislative body chosen by the voters. It is usually called a ***city council.*** The executive is usually called a ***mayor.*** There are also departments that perform the day-to-day jobs of city government.

The most common type of government is the mayor-council form. More than 75 percent of all the municipalities in Missouri use mayor-council organization. There are two basic types: one is called "weak," and the other is termed "strong." The weakness or strength is determined by how much appointive authority the mayor has. This means: Does the mayor get to appoint the police chief or other department heads, or are they elected? Does he or she have to share this appointive authority with the council?

The ***weak mayor-council form*** has the voters electing a council, a mayor, and a number of oth-

STRONG MAYOR-COUNCIL FORM

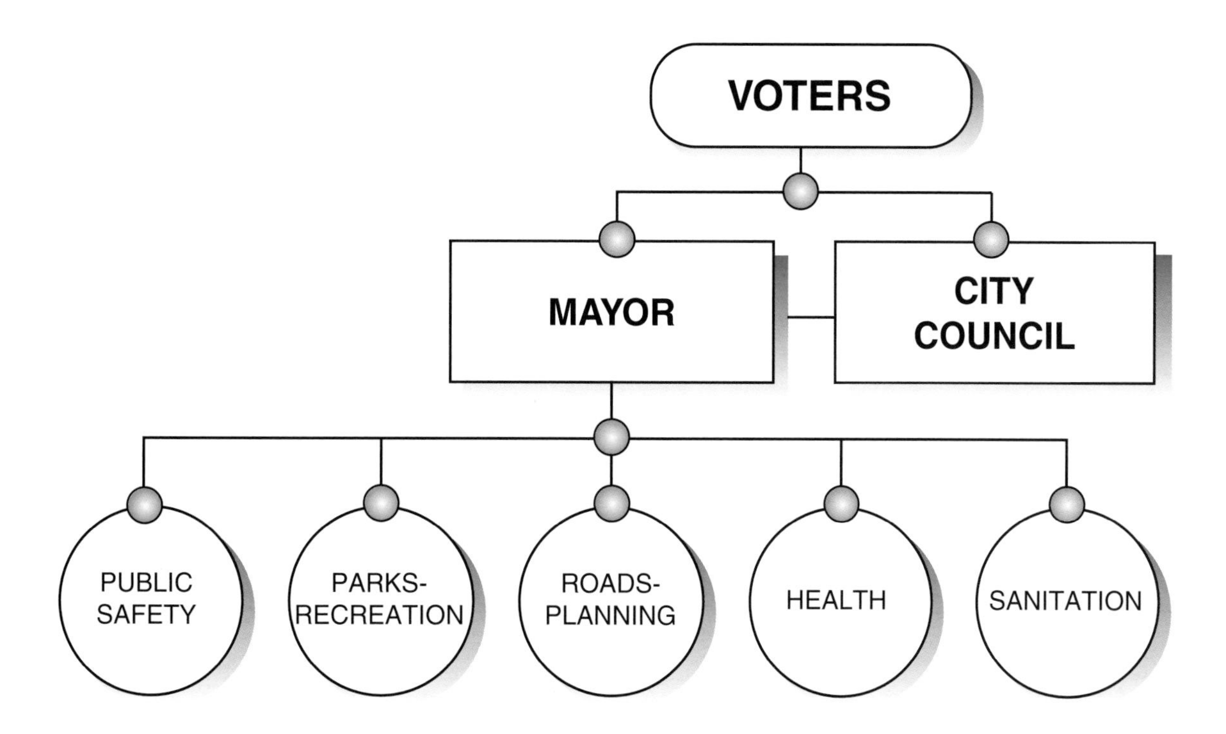

er officials. These may include a city attorney, tax collector, marshal, treasurer, assessor, and others. Some other officials may be appointed by the council; others are appointed by the mayor with the approval of the council. The mayor has little real power to act as an executive in the city. The result is that no one can be held responsible for what happens in the city government. It is difficult for one elected official to supervise another. Some people may be given jobs for political reasons in this form of government. More than half of the municipalities in our state have a weak mayor-council government. This is because the state law requires many municipalities to have several elected officials instead of appointed ones.

The ***strong mayor-council*** form puts more power in the hands of the mayor. This form, however, is available only to home rule charter cities. In this form, voters choose or elect fewer officials. The voters select a mayor and a council called a ***board of aldermen.*** Voters may elect a few other officials, or they may be appointed by the mayor. The mayor is then allowed to appoint most executive officials such as the assessor, city attorney, tax collector, clerk, and street commissioner. The result is that it is difficult to hold any one responsible for what happens in the city government. This form of government must be approved by the voters.

Small towns or villages have another form of municipal government. Here the voters elect a council called a ***board of trustees***. The board chooses a chairman and appoints all other city officials, including a marshal, tax collector, and treasurer.

Another type of organization that may be adopted is called the ***city administrator form.*** It retains the decentralized weak mayor form, but allows the mayor and council to appoint a city administrator. The city administrator works on authority

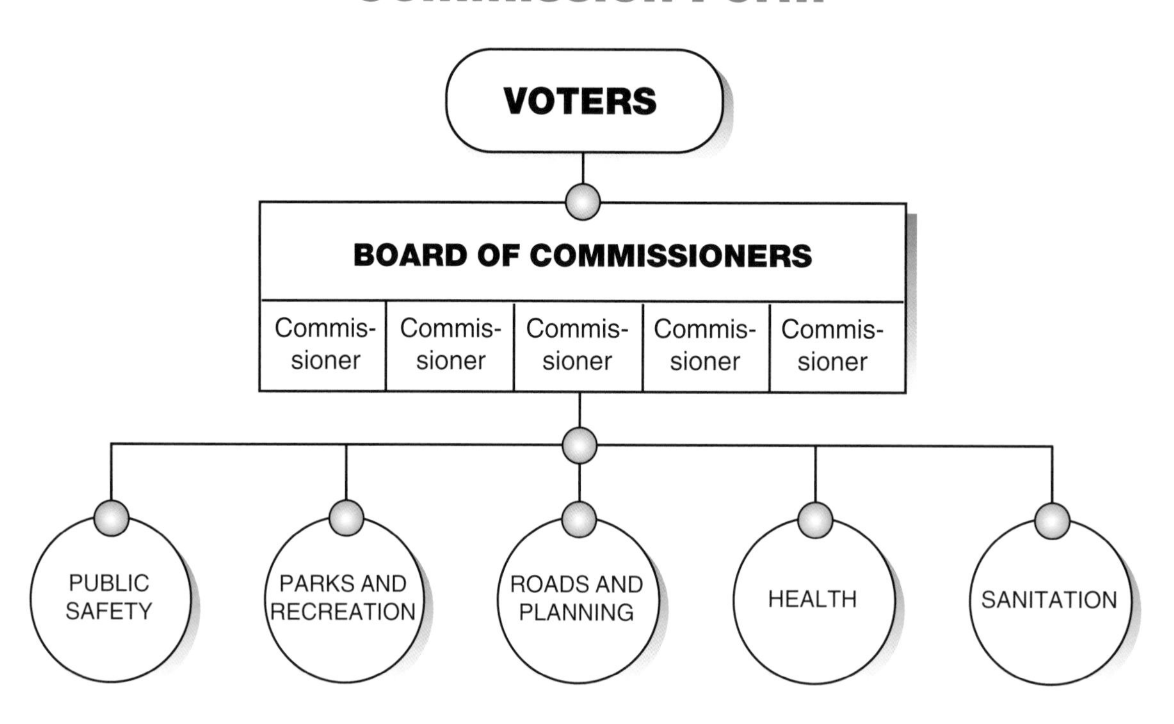
Commission Form
VOTERS
BOARD OF COMMISSIONERS
Commis-sioner
Commis-sioner
Commis-sioner
Commis-sioner
Commis-sioner
PUBLIC SAFETY
PARKS AND RECREATION
ROADS AND PLANNING
HEALTH
SANITATION

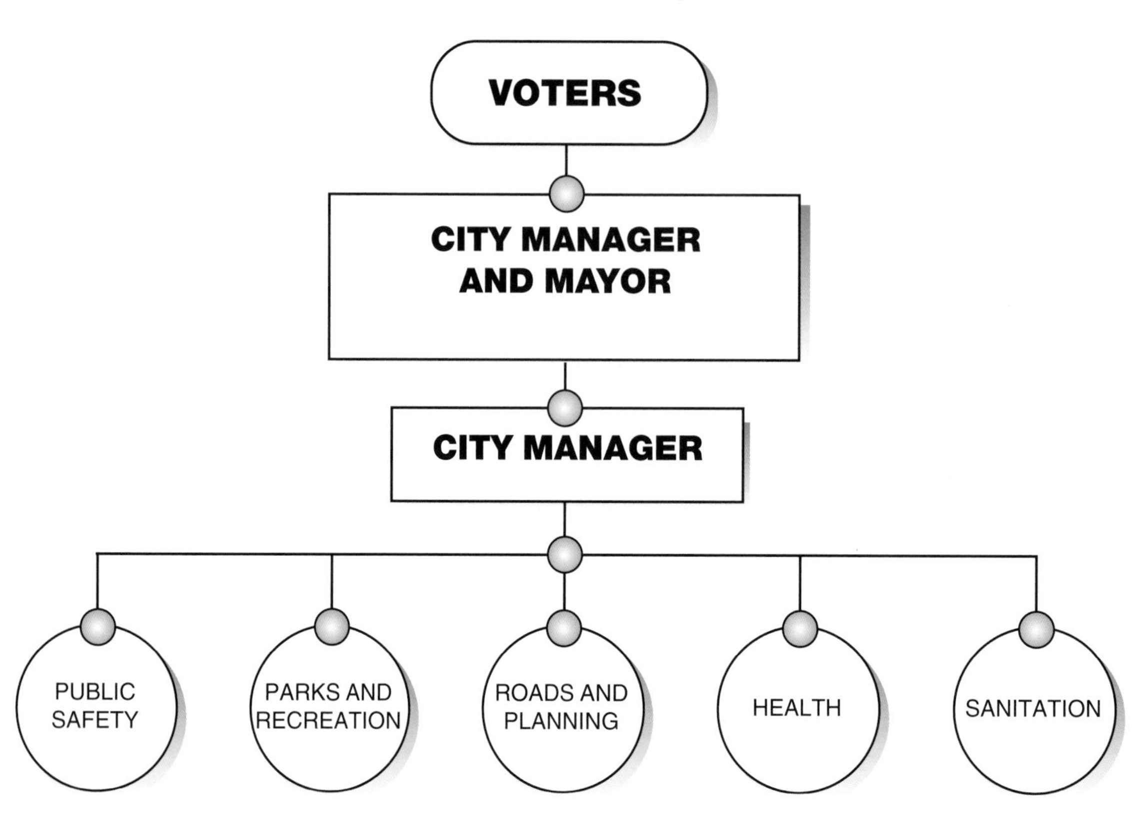
City Manager
VOTERS
CITY MANAGER AND MAYOR
CITY MANAGER
PUBLIC SAFETY
PARKS AND RECREATION
ROADS AND PLANNING
HEALTH
SANITATION

delegated by the mayor. This form has become increasingly popular because it retains the traditional weak mayor structure while providing for professional management. This can be done by ordinance rather than election, which makes abandonment easy.

The other professional management structure, the ***city manager form,*** must be approved in a citywide election and retained for at least six years. Many city populations oppose the city manager form as being dictatorial. The total number of municipalities with city managers has remained almost constant for decades. In contrast, city administrator communities are increasing and have more than doubled the number of manager cities.

The ***city council form*** of city government is used in more than 30 cities, but must be approved by the voters before it can be used. The voters elect a council and a mayor. The council members then choose a clerk, assessor, treasurer, and a manager. This council determines the policies to be followed by the city and approves the budget. The manager is trained in running the day-to-day business of the city and makes recommendations for action to the council. The manager may be fired by the council if a majority of the council members do not like his or her work. The manager appoints all other officials in the city government.

One advantage of this form of government is that patronage is less likely. Patronage is appointing political friends to jobs in government. As a result, those who run the city's business are professionals at their jobs, due to the merit system.

A very different form of government called the ***commission form*** may also be used. Voters elect the mayor and council members in an at-large election; that is, all voters in the city vote for all members of the council. The council is called a commission and each member of the commission heads at least one department of the city. The mayor also heads a department, usually the department of public affairs. Fewer than ten municipalities in Missouri use this form of government. It also requires that the elected commissioners be good administrators. A person may do a good job at representing the voters and not be a good executive.

Q:

What are the basic characteristics of each of the forms of municipal government?

DISCUSSION: WHAT ARE THE ADVANTAGES AND DISADVANTAGES OF EACH FORM OF MUNICIPAL GOVERNMENT?

SPECIAL DISTRICTS

Special districts are units of local government that are separate from municipalities or counties. They usually perform one kind of service.

These districts may cross the boundaries of both cities and unincorporated areas. Special districts handle such services as fire protection, sewers, storm drainage, and education. They are created because some other kind of government is not meeting a need of the people. Special districts usually have an elected governing body. People often know very little about these groups; thus, voter turnout at their elections may be very low. Such districts have the power to set their own taxes and make some rules.

School Districts

Public schools in Missouri are run by local ***school districts.*** There are more than 550 such districts in our state. Some provide education for kindergarten students through the 12th grade. Others may serve only through grades six or eight.

State law sets some rules to be followed by school districts. There is a state board of education that helps administer those rules. The members of this board are appointed by the governor and confirmed by the Senate. The state board appoints a commissioner of education to administer the state department of education.

Local school districts have the power to actually run the schools. Each district covers a fairly small area. A ***governing board*** is elected by the voters of the district. These boards may have between six and 12 members elected for three-year terms. The governing board sets the policies to be followed in the district.

The board sets a property tax to help pay for the cost of public schools. This local tax, plus county money, totals about 35 percent of what is spent for education. The state government provides more than 40 percent of the money for school districts, and the rest of the money comes from the federal government and a special sales tax. Bonds may be sold by the district to construct buildings. A ***bond*** is simply a promise to pay back borrowed money at a certain rate of interest. A person who buys a school bond is lending money to the school district at a fixed interest rate. Education takes a large percent of all the money spent by state and local government.

The governing board also hires a ***superintendent*** to run the day-to-day business of the district. This person carries out the decisions of the board and recommends actions to it, but serves at the pleasure of the board. The superintendent appoints school principals and other district officials. Each school has a principal, often some assistant principals, and staff. The staff may consist of teachers, counselors, a nurse, bus drivers, and custodians.

Q:

The job of superintendent in a school district is much like what other official in city government. Why?

How is a school district like a city government? How is it different?

DISCUSSION: MANY PEOPLE THINK WE SHOULD GET RID OF SPECIAL DISTRICTS AND GIVE THEIR FUNCTIONS TO CITY OR COUNTY GOVERNMENT. DISCUSS BOTH THE ADVANTAGES AND DISADVANTAGES OF THIS IDEA.

❒ SUMMARY

Local government has more to do with our daily lives than any other form of government. It provides services that we count on every day, yet most people seem to pay little attention to it. Far fewer voters take part in local elections than in national elections.

There are many kinds of local governments. They include counties, different kinds of municipalities, and different kinds of special districts. The basic rules for creating and running these forms of government are set by the state. Each has some power to set its own rules within these guidelines. Voters usually have the chance to choose the legislative body of the local government. Some local governments have other elected officials as well.

The columns of the original Boone County Courthouse in Columbia were saved when the rest of the building was razed to make room for this structure, built between 1906 and 1909. An addition was constructed to the north in 1991.

Police records must be kept secured to protect both complainants and the person or persons against whom the complaint was brought.

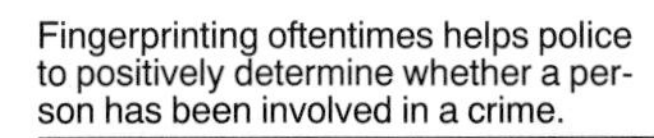

Fingerprinting oftentimes helps police to positively determine whether a person has been involved in a crime.

The City of Florissant Community Center in St. Bernard County provides indoor recreational and meeting places for individuals and groups.

REVIEW

1. Why do we have counties?
2. How are counties different from cities? How are they alike?
3. What is the purpose of a county or city charter?
4. What are the forms of municipal government in Missouri?
5. How is the executive chosen in each form of municipal government?
6. County government is organized most like which form of municipal government?
7. A city council is most like what part of the state government?
8. Why is the commission form so different from the other forms of municipal government?
9. Why do special districts exist?
10. Write a brief definition of each of the terms listed at the beginning of the chapter under "Terms to Look For."

INVESTIGATE

Facts and Figures File:
Find out the following information abut the local governments where you live. Use separate pages for county, municipality, school district, and special districts.

County
- Name of county
- Location of county seat
- Number of members on county council
- Names of other county officials and their titles
- Population of the county

Municipality
- Name of municipality
- Type of municipality (city, town, etc.)
- Form of government
- Name and title of executive
- Name of legislative branch
- Number of legislative branch members and their names
- Population of the municipality

School District
- Name of school district
- Number of members on governing board
- Kinds of schools in district (K-8, K-12)
- Number of students in district

Use your local telephone directory to identify the local government services available to you. What level of government provides them? Choose one of the agencies that provides these services and visit its office. Find out about the services it provides and who may receive the services. How does the agency receive its money? Who is in charge of the agency? How is that person chosen? Report to your class.

Attend a meeting of your local school governing board or city council. Write a summary of what you saw. What issues were being discussed? Who was in charge? How was the meeting run?

PROJECT

Make a chart that describes the organization of your local municipal government. Include color and label the chart at the top with the name of your municipality. Identify the elected and appointed officials and use lines to show which officials are responsible to which other officials. Include the names of the current officials. At the bottom of the chart, print the form of municipal government your town has.

POINT/COUNTERPOINT

There is argument about how best to provide for public education. Some people argue that schools should be run and financed locally. They want to continue with the local school board system. This is because the people who live in an area are more aware of local needs.

Others reply that local control and financing leads to unequal education. Poor areas are less able to provide a good education for children. They say that all schools should be supported equally. This would happen if the state and federal government provided the money and set the rules for running schools. Other reasons are also given by both groups.

Research both sides of this issue and then decide what your position will be. Be prepared to discuss your position in class.

TERMS TO LOOK FOR

- politics
- political system
- political party
- major parties
- issues
- moderate
- established
- minor parties
- patronage system
- party ticket
- party identification
- Democratic party
- Republican party
- ward
- township
- district committee
- state committee
- committeemen
- committeewomen
- county central committees
- lobbyists
- party platform
- PACs
- elections
- plurality
- nominee
- open primary
- electorate
- national requirements
- literacy tests
- residence requirement
- Missouri requirements
- precinct
- polling place
- polls
- election judge
- ballot

6

The Missouri Political System

Politics is a word that is often seen in the newspaper. It simply means the art of getting and using power. It is the grease that allows the wheels of government to turn. ***Politics*** is a part of any group; it is not just used in government. Certain people become leaders of a group and get the rest of its members to follow. There are several different ideas and groups that are part of the art of politics; together they are the political system. Political parties are a big part of the ***political system.*** They are organizations that choose candidates and try to get them elected. We have two large political parties and some smaller ones. There are other groups that try to help certain candidates get elected. They are called interest groups. Interest groups want to influence public policy through public or private activities. They do not often run their own candidates in an election. When they do, it is never under the label of their organization. Holding an elective office might hinder that group in its private efforts to influence public policy and to gain access to all politicians. Elections are the means we use to choose which candidate will hold each elected office. Primary elections are used by political parties to choose their candidates. General elections choose which party candidate will fill each elected office. Winners in these elections are the candidates with the most votes. Special elections may be held for special purposes. The people are the key to making our government work. The political system is the means the people have of controlling their government. Being a citizen requires that each person be aware of what is happening in government. A citizen needs to pay attention to the campaigns of candidates for office. What do they stand for? What are their ideas about what government should do? Finally, a citizen must take the time to go to the polls and vote. How well our government serves us depends on each of us participating in the political system.

Political Parties and Interest Groups

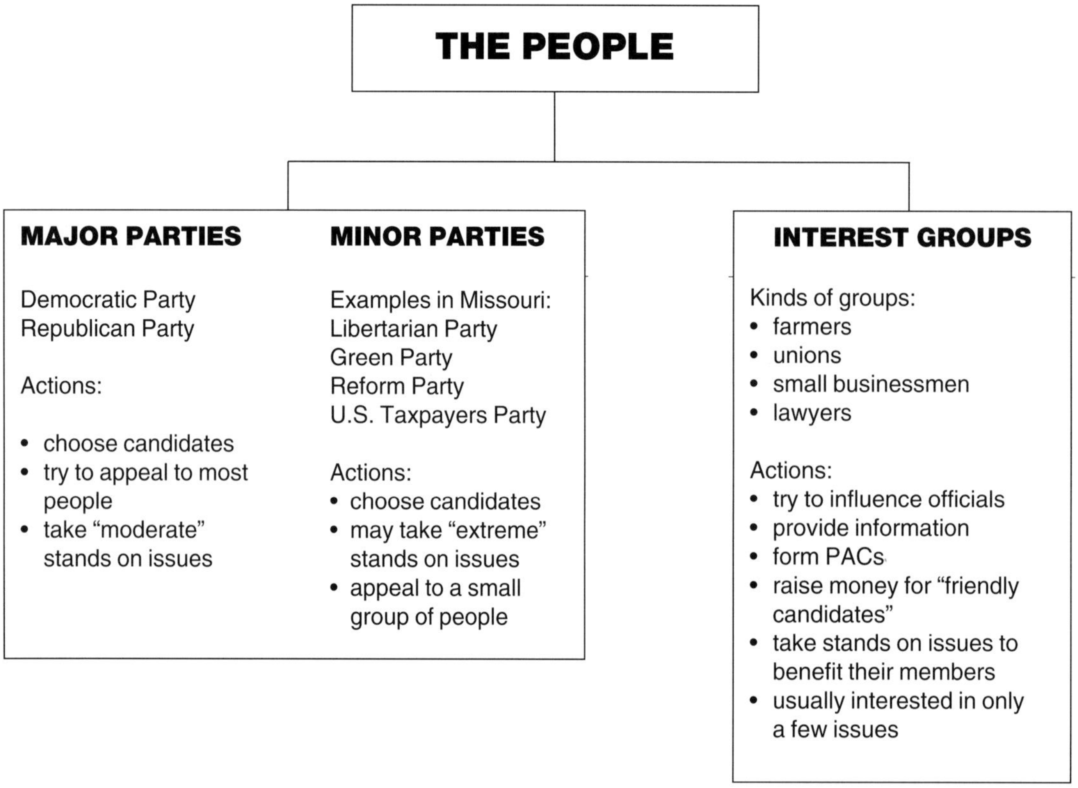

THE PEOPLE

MAJOR PARTIES	**MINOR PARTIES**	**INTEREST GROUPS**
Democratic Party Republican Party Actions: • choose candidates • try to appeal to most people • take "moderate" stands on issues	Examples in Missouri: Libertarian Party Green Party Reform Party U.S. Taxpayers Party Actions: • choose candidates • may take "extreme" stands on issues • appeal to a small group of people	Kinds of groups: • farmers • unions • small businessmen • lawyers Actions: • try to influence officials • provide information • form PACs • raise money for "friendly candidates" • take stands on issues to benefit their members • usually interested in only a few issues

POLITICAL PARTIES

A ***political party*** is an organized group whose purpose is to choose candidates for office and try to get them elected. A person may become a member of a political party by simply saying he or she is a member. There are no required meetings or dues. There are two basic types of political parties. They are major and minor parties.

Major parties try to appeal to a large number of people. They do this by talking about many different ***issues.*** Such issues might be taxes, education, pollution, and jobs in our state. People who think of themselves as members of a political party may disagree with other members on some issues and agree on others. The major parties try not to be considered "extreme" on issues. They take stands on issues that are considered ***moderate*** or "middle of the road." The voters think of major parties as "acceptable."

The Democrats and the Republicans are the major parties in Missouri and the rest of the country. These parties do not have to get signatures on petitions in order to get their candidates on the ballot. They are considered ***established*** by law in the state.

Minor parties are a little different. They also choose candidates for office and work to get them elected. However, they do not appeal to as large a number of people as the major parties. The reason for this is that they take stands on issues with which many people disagree. They often will stress only one issue in a campaign. Many people may consider their position to be "extreme." The result is that minor parties tend to appeal to a single group of people. There is little room for those who disagree on that one issue. Minor parties do not often win elections because they do not appeal to a large percent of the people. They may see their job to be bringing up ideas that the major parties believe are unpopular. Major parties may then pick up the idea if it becomes popular. The minor party would then no longer have reason to exist. Minor parties may also be set up around a single candidate for office.

It is difficult for minor parties to get on the ballot. For a new party to be formed statewide, a petition with at least 10,000 signatures of registered voters must be filed with the secretary of state. At the district or county level, a new party must get a petition signed by registered voters equaling two percent of the vote in the last election for the office being sought—or 10,000 voters, whichever is less. At its first election, a newly formed party can become "established" with more than two percent of the total vote. In statewide elections, if the minor party fails to have a candidate for two consecutive elections, the party is no longer "established."

Q:

What is the purpose of political parties?

What is the difference between a major and a minor party?

DISCUSSION: WHAT WOULD HAPPEN IF MISSOURI HAD ONLY ONE POLITICAL PARTY?

HOW COULD MINOR PARTIES SUCCEED IN WINNING ELECTIONS? WHAT WOULD HAPPEN THEN?

Political Parties in Missouri's History

The dominant political party in Missouri has been the Democrats, although this is beginning to change. The Missouri General Assembly was dominated by Democrat's in the 20th century. State offices have also been held by Demo-crats for most of the time. However, voters have learned to split tickets and vote for Republicans, at least at the state level. Republicans captured all but one of the state offices in 1988, only to lose them to the Democrats in 1992. In 2002 Republicans gained control of the General Assembly and the second U.S. Senate seat.

Missouri parties have had little success in Missouri elections throughout its history. One reason is that they must become "established" in order to be on the ballot without getting many petitions signed. Another is that their issues have not appealed to a number of different groups of people. A minor party has not elected a member of the General Assembly since 1914. A minor party has never received a vote for President from Missouri in the electoral college.

There were some minor parties in the late 1800s that gained some support. These parties were supported by farmers protesting poor farming conditions. They included the People's Party, Greenback Party, Greenback Labor Party, and Union Labor Party. None of them won control of the state government. They did succeed in getting the major parties to pay attention to their issues. These included low prices for farm products, high interest rates on loans, and high railroad freight rates.

Political parties do not now hold the power over elections that they once did. There are many reasons for this. People do not have to register as Republicans or Democrats. They may vote in the primary election of either party. Many candidates do not need party help to campaign because they have their own organizations. They appeal directly to voters through television. They stress ideas instead of party label. Candidates take public opinion polls to see how people feel about issues. Then they take stands on these issues. The result is that the party is not as needed to help the candidate get elected.

Most state workers are protected from the old ***patronage system***. That is, they can no longer be hired and fired for political reasons. Candidates who win elections cannot reward the party workers with jobs. This gives the party less power in running the government.

Many voters no longer vote a straight ***party ticket.*** It does not allow a voter to make one mark to vote for all the candidates on one party. There has been a decline in voter ***party identification*** in recent years. Many people do not see themselves as loyal members of either major party. Voters do not seem to identify with any of the minor parties either. Being "independent" may have become the trend in voting.

Q:

Why did patronage help give power to political parties?

Why are political parties less powerful today than they once were?

DISCUSSION: WHY DID MISSOURI'S MINOR POLITICAL PARTIES DIE OUT DURING THE EARLIER HISTORY?

The Major Parties

Both the Democrats and Republicans try to appeal to a large number of different people. For this reason it is not possible to say that one group supports the Democrats and the other supports the Republicans. There are some general trends, however. These trends do not look at individual voters. Instead they consider millions of voters across the nation.

The ***Democratic Party*** in Missouri has had the most success in the past in getting its candidates elected. Across the nation, the Democratic party has seemed to have had the most appeal to certain groups. These tend to include union members, ethnic minorities, city voters, and the poor. The Democrats show the most strength in Missouri in Jackson County (Kansas City) and St. Louis. Democrats have favored collective bargaining for public employees. This would allow government workers to form unions and bargain for wage increases. Democrats have also supported using tax money to clean up water pollution in the state.

The ***Republican Party*** had very limited success in Missouri until the 1980s. Across the nation, the Republicans seem to appeal most to professional people, majority group voters, suburban voters, successful farmers, and businessmen. Republican strength in Missouri is shown in the northwestern and southwestern parts of the state. Republicans have opposed collective bargaining for public employees in the state. They also have supported laws to encourage new business in Missouri.

These descriptions of Democrats and Republicans are very general. Many voters today vote more for individual candidates and not for the party. This means that parties must choose strong candidates in order to have them elected. They cannot depend on the party label to attract votes.

DISCUSSION: HOW ARE THE DEMOCRATIC AND REPUBLICAN PARTIES DIFFERENT? HOW ARE THEY SIMILAR?

Minor Parties Today

Few minor parties have been on the ballot in recent years, although the Libertarian party is state recognized, or established. In 1992, it had candidates for President and Vice President, U.S. Senator, Lieutenant Governor, Secretary of State, State Treasurer, and Attorney General. It also had

Political Parties and Interest Groups

STATE COMMITTEE

- write party platform
- plan election campaign
- raise money
- work with county and district committees

DISTRICT COMMITTEE

- choose man and woman to serve on state committee
- choose replacement candidates for General Assembly
- choose replacement candidate for some judgeships

COUNTY COMMITTEE

- help elect local candidates
- keep local headquarters
- register voters
- choose poll watchers
- organize campaign rallies
- choose replacement candidates for county offices
- choose members of district committee

WARD OR TOWNSHIP

- committee: man and woman
- conduct local campaign
- find workers for polls

candidates in two congressional district races, one state senate race, and 13 house contests. However, it had no winners. Its state headquarters is located in Springfield in southwest Missouri, which is a strong conservative Republican area.

Other minor parties represented in the 1992 general election were the Natural Law and Green parties, which also had no winners. Others, such as the Citizens party, which had a candidate for the state Senate in 1980, are no longer established. They did not receive enough votes to remain on the ballot in 1982. The Socialist Workers party suffered the same fate. Independents also ran in several races. Surprisingly, Ross Perot, as an independent, received more than 20 percent of the state's vote for President in 1992.

Party Organization

Established political parties have set up many different groups to help with their work. Each group is organized at a different level. Some are statewide and some are local. Each group has certain jobs to do; they are called the party organization. Both established parties have created these groups.

> **Q:**
>
> Why do major parties have an advantage over minor ones by being called "established"?

Ward or township. *Wards* and *townships* are local areas. There are a total of 1,768 in the state. Each such local area may elect one man and one woman to work for each major party in that area. Their titles are committeeman and committeewoman. State law requires that there be an equal number of men and women in the party committee structure. These people run the party's local campaign. They also find people to work for the party at the polls on election day. People who fill these jobs are elected at a primary election. Both parties often have trouble finding people to serve as *committeemen* and *committeewomen.* The only qualification is to be a registered voter.

County committee. The local committee persons set up county central committees. Each county committee chooses four officers: a chairperson, a vice chairperson, a secretary, and a treasurer. *County central committees* do many jobs, like:

- Help elect local party candidates
- Maintain a local party headquarters
- Organize drives to register voters
- Choose "poll watchers" to watch the voting and vote counting on election day to make sure it is fair
- Organize rallies for candidates
- Choose new candidates for county office if one cannot run in an election
- Choose persons to serve on the district committee

Rallies are exciting events to "kick off" campaigns for political candidates—and for the people who will work to help them win the election.

District committee. District committees serve both major parties between the county and state levels. There are only four kinds of district committees: legislative, senatorial, judicial, and congressional.

- The legislative district committee may name a new candidate for the state House of Representatives. This could happen if the first candidate cannot run.
- The senatorial district committee does the same thing for state Senate jobs. It also chooses a man and a woman to serve on the party's state committee.
- The judicial district committee may put a new candidate on the ballot for circuit judge. Again, this could happen if the first nominated candidate cannot run. It cannot be used for those circuits that use the Non-Partisan Court Plan.
- The congressional district committees nominate two voters from each congressional district to serve on another committee. It is called the House redistricting committee. This is the group that redraws district boundary lines for members of the U.S. House of Representatives from Missouri. The governor will choose half of the people nominated by the two parties to serve on the redistricting committee.

State Committee. Each major party has a state committee. It is made up of one member from each state senate district. Some of the jobs done by this committee include:

- putting together the state ***party platform.*** The platform is a list of general statements of what the party stands for.
- planning the party campaign in a general election.
- raising money.
- working with county and district committees.

DISCUSSION: IDENTIFY IN ONE OR TWO SENTENCES FOR EACH, THE PURPOSE OF THE DIFFERENT LEVELS OF PARTY ORGANIZATION.

INTEREST GROUPS

Interest groups are formed by people who have a common goal. They share an idea or something they want the government to do. Interest groups usually center around one point of view on one or a few issues. They work to get that point of view accepted as government policy. Interest groups try to influence those who hold political office, They seldom try to run their own candidates. Most often an interest group will try to influence the legislature.

Interest groups try to influence government in many ways. They often have one or more people who represent them in talking to officials. They are called ***lobbyists.*** This term came from the fact that many years ago they would wait in the lobby of the congress or state legislature to see representatives and senators. Members of interest groups may be asked to write letters to members of the legislature to express their points of view. Interest groups may also advertise their ideas in the media.

Interest groups almost always raise money to help candidates who are friendly to their point of view. This money is raised and spent by groups that are many times called political action committees, or ***PACs***. PACs have become a major source of money for many candidates running for office. They have even supported an initiative or referendum campaign to change a law.

There are several types of interest groups. Some support a point of view on economic issues. Others want to influence public policy on social issues. Still others work for a unit of government, such as a county or city.

There are more economic interest groups than any other kind. Such groups represent the points of view of many different interests. Examples are interest groups that represent farmers, industries, labor unions, professional groups, real estate sales, and small businesses. Economic interest groups are normally the most powerful type of interest group in a state.

Another type of interest group tries to influence the social policy of government. They could be called social interest groups. Many of them support certain ideas about moral issues. Examples of these issues are abortion, racial equality, prayer in school, and the death penalty. Some of these groups want new laws on such topics as pollution, drunk driving, and protection of wild animals.

A third type of interest group works for other levels of government. A group may represent school districts that want more money from the state for education. Another may represent cities and towns that want more help to build roads, parks, or playgrounds. Most of these groups want to get more money from the legislature for their level of government.

Q:

How are interest groups different from political parties?

DISCUSSION: ARE INTEREST GROUPS A GOOD OR BAD INFLUENCE ON GOVERNMENT?

Types of Elections in Missouri

TYPE OF ELECTION	PURPOSE(S)	WHEN
Primary	Nominate candidates for offices	August of even-numbered years
General	Choose officials for government	November of even-numbered years
Special	Fill vacancy in office Approve school taxes or bonds	As needed
Local	Choose city, town, or district officials	Often in April

Voting Population in Missouri by Age Group 2000

Age	Percent of Voting-Age Population
18-24	13%
25-44	39%
45-64	30%
65+	18%

Voter Turnout

Percent of voting-age population that voted

	National	Missouri
1996:	49%	54%
2000:	50%	57%

ELECTIONS

Elections are one of the main ways citizens can control their government. Elections are used at all levels of government to choose who will serve as officials. In most cases, the winner of an election is the person with more votes than any other candidate. Having more votes than any other candidate is called having a ***plurality.*** Suppose that there are more than two candidates in an election. The winner will be the one with the highest number of votes. There are many different kinds of elections used in Missouri.

Primary Elections

Primaries are elections within a political party. A party uses a primary to choose who will be its candidates. The candidate in a primary who has the plurality becomes the party's ***nominee*** for the office. Primary elections take place on the first Tuesday after the first Monday in August of the even-numbered years. Candidates are chosen at that time for offices that will be filled in the general election in November of the same year.

Missouri uses the ***open primary*** system. This means that a voter may choose in which party's primary to vote. A voter does this by taking the ballot of one party when he or she goes to vote in the primary. In many states, a voter may vote only in the primary of the party in which he or she is registered. This is called a "closed" primary.

General Elections

In the general election, the candidates nominated in the primary run against each other. The candidate winning this election serves a term in the office being chosen. The winner is decided by a plurality vote. For example, suppose there were three candidates in the general election for governor, and that the Democratic candidate received 34 percent of the vote. If the Republican candidate received 33 percent of the vote and the Libertarian candidate received the other 33 percent, the Democratic candidate would be elected to office. If there is a tie in the vote for an office, a new election would be called. This almost never happens.

General elections take place on the first Tuesday after the first Monday in November of the even-numbered years. Candidates are chosen to fill the offices of those whose terms are ended at that time. Some offices are open for election every two years. Examples are members of the U.S. House of Representatives and the House in the state legislature. Every four years, many other offices are also filled. These include governor and the other state executive offices, presidential electors, and state senators.

Other Elections

Special elections may be called for several reasons. They are used to fill a vacancy in an office because of the death or resignation of an official. They are also used to approve a school levy (tax) or bond. Elections to fill positions in cities and on school boards are often held in April.

> **Q:**
>
> What are the differences between the types of elections?

DISCUSSION: WHAT WOULD HAPPEN IF THERE WERE NO PRIMARIES AND ALL CANDIDATES SIMPLY RAN IN THE GENERAL ELECTION?

WOULD IT BE MORE OR LESS DEMOCRATIC TO HOLD ALL OF THE "OTHER ELECTIONS" AT THE TIME OF THE GENERAL ELECTION? WHY?

THE ELECTORATE

The ***electorate*** is made up of all qualified voters. Both the national and state governments have rules about who may vote.

National requirements

- The minimum age by law cannot be higher than 18.
- Race, color, or sex cannot be used to stop a person from voting.
- No ***literacy tests*** can be used in registering voters. This means that no tests may be required to see if a voter can read or write. The courts have held that these tests are unconstitutional.
- A voter cannot be required to live in a state longer than 50 days before being able to register to vote. This is called a ***residence requirement.***

Missouri requirements

- A voter must be a U.S. citizen.
- A voter must ***register*** to vote. A political party preference does not need to be given. The purpose of registration is to prevent cheating on election day. Voters may register at the Board of Election Commissioners in their county or other places that are provided, such as a library, school, or even specially equipped vans.
- A voter must re-register if he or she changes his/her name or address, or fails to vote at least once in four years.
- A person is disqualified from voting if convicted of a felony or of a misdemeanor connected with election laws.

> **Q:**
>
> How would you describe a person who is qualified to vote in Missouri? Include all of the requirements for voting.

Schools, community buildings, and churches are probably the most often used structures for polling places. But even mobile vans are used in some areas where people can't easily get to the polls.

VOTING

Citizens vote at a special place in a small area around where they live. This area is called a ***precinct.*** The place where a person actually votes is called a ***polling place.*** The polling place may be in a school, community building, church, or other place that has enough space. The room where voting takes place is often called the ***polls.***

There are several officials in each polling place on election day. At least four official ***election judges*** are used. An equal number of Democratic and Republican judges are there. They handle the official ballots and actually conduct the voting. There are also two supervisors: one Republican and one Democrat. They watch to make sure that there is no cheating.

A voter must sign a signature card before receiving a ***ballot***. Three systems of voting and two kinds of ballots are presently in use in Missouri. Some election districts use the old fashioned lever voting machines, which don't use a ballot. On an individual machine, the voter turns small levers next to the names of candidates or issues. The machine tallies the totals, which are read at the closing of the polls. Many larger population districts use punch card ballots counted by machines. The voter uses a stylus to punch a hole in the card by the names of favored candidates or issues. The third type, which is increasing in popularity, is the optical scanner similar to those in grocery stores. Ballots for scanners are similar to multiple choice tests: a special pencil is used for marking and a scanner reads the ballots.

Q:

How would you explain in your own words what happens when a citizen goes to vote?

Political Citizenship

Register to Vote

Find out about the Issues

Talk with Others

Contact Officials

Attend Meetings

POLITICAL CITIZENSHIP

Voting is an important part of being a citizen in the United States. Many people do not use their right to vote. Then they may want to complain about what government does. A citizen in a democracy can do several things to have an effect on the government.

The first step is to register to vote. Without this, a citizen's voice cannot be heard in elections. The next important task of political citizenship is to know the issues that are important in an election. Read the newspapers and watch news on television. Try to hear candidates speak in person if possible. Discuss the issues with friends and family. Find out how the issues affect you and the people around you. Decide with which candidates you agree the most.

When you are able to vote, take the time to go to the polls on election day! After the election, follow what is happening in government through the news. Then when you go to vote the next time, remember what officials have done that you do or do not like. An informed public that participates in voting is the key to a political system that works for the people.

There are other ways to make your voice heard by government, too. Contact your public officials. Let them know what you think. You should do this if you believe a person is doing a good job, as well as if you disagree. If officials hear only from those who complain, they may be forced to change their ideas. You can contact elected officials by telephone, letter, telegrams, or even an office visit, to tell them your opinions. You can also attend meetings, hearings, and presentations. Many of these allow time for the public to speak. You will also learn a lot about what goes into making decisions about public issues.

DISCUSSION: IN WHAT AREAS OF YOUR LIFE AND THAT OF YOUR FAMILY DO POLITICAL DECISIONS HAVE THE MOST DIRECT EFFECT? GIVE EXAMPLES.

WHAT COULD YOU DO TO HAVE AN EFFECT ON THOSE DECISIONS?

❐ SUMMARY

The political system is the "grease" that makes the machine of government work. This system is made up of many different parts. Political parties choose candidates and try to get them elected. Major political parties try to appeal to a large number of different people. The Democratic and Republican parties are the major parties in Missouri and in the United States. They win almost all of the elections. Minor parties often appeal to a much smaller group. They may take a stand on issues with which most people do not agree. The major parties will likely adopt the ideas of a minor party if it is successful. The result is that the minor party still does not get candidates elected to office. Political parties are very loosely organized. They have groups set up to work at the ward, county, district, and state levels in Missouri.

Interest groups try to influence those who are elected. Each is interested only in certain issues. People who work for interest groups to contact officials are call lobbyists. Interest groups create PACs to raise money for campaigns of friendly officials who are up for election.

Elections give the citizens a chance to control their government. Most elections are won by a plurality of the vote. Primary elections choose party candidates for office. General elections decide which candidates will hold the office. Other elections are held for many different reasons. These may include filling a vacant office, approving bonds or taxes, and for local offices.

A person must meet certain qualifications to be able to vote. These are set by both the national and state governments. The qualifications include age, residence, and registration. There can be no qualifications to vote dealing with race, sex, color, or literacy. Voters must re-register if they change their name or address or fail to vote every four years.

Each voter lives in a voting precinct with a polling place. Several officials run each polling place. Voters use either a lever voting machine, or paper or machine ballots to indicate their election choices. Almost half of Missouri counties still use paper ballots, the oldest form. Ballots counted by scanners are gaining in popularity.

Voting is the central part of political citizenship in this country. Keeping up on the issues and candidates through the news media is needed to be able to decide how to vote. Democracy works only when the citizens use their opportunity to participate in government.

REVIEW

1. What are the functions of a political party?
2. Why has Missouri been called a "Democratic state" in the past?
3. What is the effect on political parties of the voters being more independent?
4. How would you describe the Republican and Democratic parties in Missouri?
5. What are the functions of minor parties in Missouri?
6. What are the four levels of party organization? What is done by each?
7. Why do interest groups exist?
8. What are the two major types of elections in Missouri? What is the function of each?
9. What are the qualifications to vote in Missouri?
10. What are the different ways in which a citizen may make his or her opinions known to government on political issues?
11. Write a brief definition of each of the terms listed at the beginning of the chapter under "Terms To Look For."

INVESTIGATE

Facts and Figures File:
Find out the names of all the minor political parties that exist today in Missouri. Make a chart with the names of each across the top. Under each name, list the following information:

- The issues in which the party is interested and its positions on these issues
- The offices for which it has run candidates recently
- The kinds of groups that have supported the party (farmers, labor, etc.)
- The name(s) of the party leaders
- Where the party headquarters is located
- Ties that party has to interest groups and other political parties

What political part is strongest in your area? Why is this true?

PROJECT

This project involves finding out what makes a political party tick. First, choose a political party—one of the major parties or a minor party—with which to work. Then, find out the names of local political party leaders. They may be state or county, district leaders, or a local committeeman or committeewoman. Contact one of the people who works for the party you have chosen and set up an interview. At the interview, ask the person to talk to you about

- the jobs they do for the party.
- why they want to work for the party.
- what they see as the main purpose of the party.
- the issues in which the party is interested.
- why the party has or has not had success in recent elections.

When you have completed your interview, write an essay to summarize what you learned. Then make a presentation to your class about what you found.

POINT/COUNTERPOINT

The media, especially television, are now a large part of a political campaign. This is why campaigns cost so much money today. The result is that a candidate for statewide office must raise a great deal of money in order to have a chance to win an election. Many people believe that something should be done to limit the amount of money spent on campaigns. In fact, Missouri has made a law to attempt to do just that. Other people argue that the media help citizens find out about the candidates and issues. They say that without this kind of campaign, fewer people would vote, and those who do vote would not be as informed about the issues. People today learn about current events mainly through television.

Choose one side of this issue or the other. Then do some research on the issue. Talk to political party workers and/or candidates. Talk to your neighbors to find out how they get information about candidates and political issues. Write an essay that supports the side you have taken. In your essay, be sure to include

- a paragraph at the beginning that states the problem.
- some paragraphs that describe your opinion and the reasons for it.
- a paragraph at the end that draws a conclusion.

Finally, get together with others in your class who took the same position that you took. Put all of your information together. Then debate the issue in front of the class with someone from the other side of the issue.

TERMS TO LOOK FOR

- goods
- services
- production
- distribution
- factors of production
- natural resources
- human resources
- capital resources
- technology
- productivity
- investment
- specialization
- population
- demographics
- ethnic minorities
- trade
- work force
- per capita
- gross state product
- service industries
- recession
- depression

7

The Missouri Economy

The economy of a state has two parts: the production and distribution of what is made in the state. Both goods and services are produced in our state. ***Goods*** are things that are produced, such as cars, books, and ice cream. ***Services*** are what a person does to accomplish something. Car repair, typing, and teaching are examples of services. ***Production*** is the making of goods and services. ***Distribution*** refers to who is able to get the goods and services that are produced. The industries in a state that produce goods and services are a big part of the state's economy. Manufacturing, construction, agriculture, tourism, and mining are major industries in Missouri. Another important part of the Missouri economy is the people who live here. How old are they? How many are retired? How many are employed? What kind of education and training do they have? Are they union members? What is the average family income? The answers to these and other questions help to shape the state's economy. How the land of the state is used is also important to the state's economy. Can much of it be used for agriculture? Is water available? Who owns the land? What kinds of minerals are available as natural resources? Government can affect the economy, although most of the action is with private business. Government contracts are important for some industries. Boeing Corporation in St. Louis, for example, is very important to the defense industry by producing fighter aircraft for the Navy and Air Force. State governments also attempt to help the economy by attracting new businesses to the state and expanding those already in operation. Healthy and expanding economies create new jobs and reduce unemployment. In that way, state and local revenues are also increased without tax increases. Missouri has been known for low taxes throughout its history. Some people argue that low taxes have not helped the economy as much as expected, but Missourians generally dislike big government and taxes.

PRODUCTION AND DISTRIBUTION

How goods are produced is important to the state's economy. Goods are made by combining three *factors of production.*These factors are natural resources, human resources, and capital resources.

Natural resources are things that exist in nature, such as coal, iron, and ore; or that can be grown, like cotton. Missouri has many natural resources that can be used to make goods. Industry can also bring more natural resources to Missouri from other states or foreign countries. ***Human resources*** are the efforts of people who do work of any kind. Human resources are also called "labor." The work of farmers, steelworkers, accountants, and doctors are types of human resources.

The third factor of production is ***capital resources.*** These are the machines that are used to produce goods. Human resources are needed to operate capital resources. A metal stamping machine that forms fenders for cars is an example of a capital resource. So are a dump truck, a plow, and a computer. There have been many new inventions and improvements in capital resources in recent years. These improvements in machines are called new ***technology,*** like using computers to control machines on a car assembly line. New technology allows machines and workers to make more goods and services in the same amount of time. This is called an increase in ***productivity.*** The purchase of these new machines by industry is called ***investment.*** It is done in order to be able to produce more goods and services for sale. Most of Missouri's industries use much of this new technology.

New technology has created an environment requiring that each person learns to do a specific task that most other people cannot do. This is called ***specialization.*** It results in each of us depending on others to do many tasks for us. For example, a computer programmer may hire others to repair a car, complete a tax form, or landscape his or her property. Most of us cannot learn to do the variety of jobs we need to have done today. This is because of the amount of technology that is now used. However, technology and specialization produce far more goods and services than could be accomplished without it.

Some people need to be retrained to find jobs that require knowledge of this technology. State

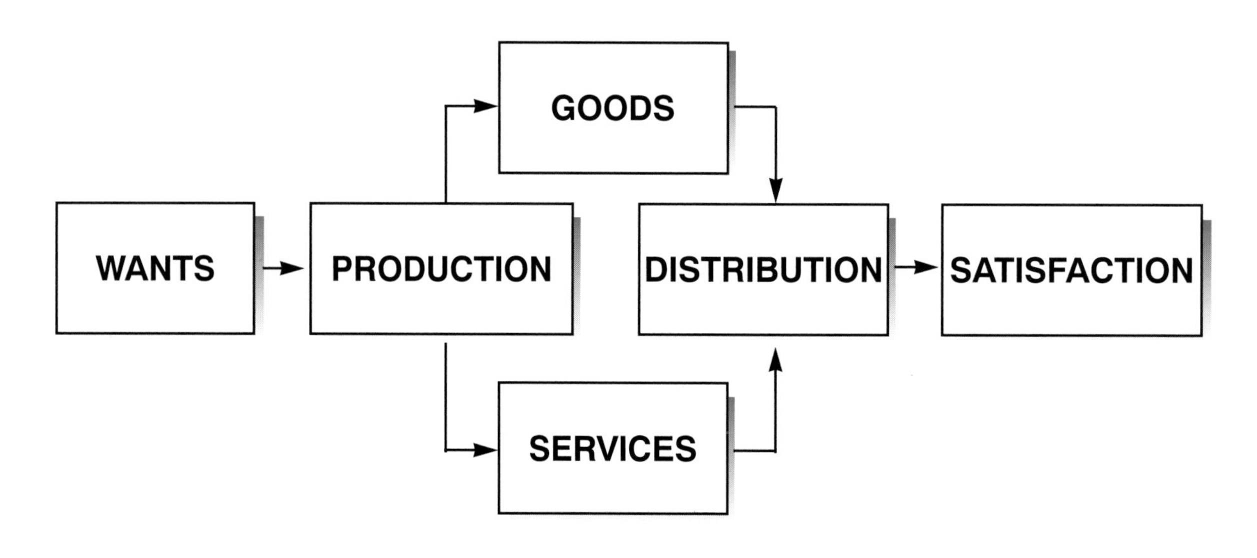

Industry and transportation stand side-by-side to produce and deliver goods quickly all over the world via highways, rails, water, and air.

and local governments often try to help them get the necessary training through the school systems and special training programs.

One of Missouri's greatest concerns, like that of any other state, is how to keep the economy growing by keeping its citizens employed. Employment gives people the ability to earn money and therefore purchase the goods and services that are produced.

Q:

What are some examples of the factors of production?

How can the factors of production be changed to produce more goods?

DISCUSSION: What benefits have come from new technology?

What problems have been created by new technology?

THE PEOPLE

There are now more than five million people who live in Missouri. Almost seventy percent of them live in the cities and suburbs. The rest live in the rural areas. The ***population*** of the state is growing, but is below the average rate of growth for the nation. The Census Bureau estimates that there were 5,629,707 residents in 2001. Much of the new growth is in cities located on the fringes of major metropolitan areas, primarily near recreation areas. This trend continues in the twenty-first century.

Several facts that describe the people of Missouri are important. These are called ***demographics.*** About 25 percent are under the age of 18. Thirteen percent are age 65 or older. This means that 62 percent of the people are in the "working age" of 18-64. According to the Census Bureau 84 percent of the population in 2000 was white, down from 88 percent in 1990. About 13 percent were ***ethnic minorities,*** with African-Americans being the largest with 11 percent. Other ethnic groups constituted about 3 percent of the population.

Workers

The workers have jobs in a number of different industries. Remember that workers are also called "human resources." About 15 percent of the people work in manufacturing. Another 12 percent are in retail ***trade.*** These people sell goods. Yet another 28 percent are in the professions. These include architects, lawyers, teachers, doctors, and others. Almost 16 percent work for a government. The rest are in other industries, or are self-employed.

Unemployment in Missouri is often less than in the nation as a whole. In April of 2003 a little over 6 percent of the work force in the nation could not find jobs. At the same time the unemployment rate for the Missouri work force was less than 5.5 percent. The ***work force*** means people who are able to work and want a job. During the ten-year period of 1984-1993, Missouri's unemployment rate was lower than that of the nation for six of those years.

Consumers

The median household income, meaning the midpoint between highest and lowest incomes, was $37,934 in 1999. The ***per capita*** income, meaning the average amount of income per person, in Missouri was $28,936 in 2002. Per capita income is calculated by dividing the total income earned by the number of people in the state. For some time, Missouri's per capita and median family incomes have been slightly below the national average. However, the cost of living in Missouri is less than in some other states, due in part to low taxation.

Workers in a meat processing plant prepare meat according to USDA standards for distribution to hotels, restaurants, and grocery stores.

DISCUSSION: WHY ARE THE CHARACTERISTICS OF THE PEOPLE IN THE STATE IMPORTANT TO THE STATE GOVERNMENT?

INDUSTRY

The gross state product in 1999 was about $163 billion. The ***gross state product*** is the total value of all goods and services produced in the state in a year. The ***service industries*** make up more than 70 percent of this amount. Service industries include wholesale and retail trade, finance, insurance, real estate, social services, transportation, utilities, and many others. The rest of the gross state product comes from manufacturing, construction, and agriculture.

Manufacturing

Education, health and social services and retail employ 32 percent of our state's work force. Fifteen percent of Missouri's work force is engaged in manufacturing. Some of the products made in Missouri include cars, aircraft, military aircraft, missiles, machinery, beer, chemicals, metal products, electronics, and glass. The manufacturing centers are St. Louis and Kansas City.

The world's largest brewer is located in St. Louis. It is the Anheuser-Busch company. The Boeing Corporation is a major employer in the state. The company makes aircraft, missiles, and electronic products at its St. Louis operation. Other big employers in the state include food produc-

Making Economic Decisions

STEPS	EXAMPLE
1. **Decide on a goal**	1. Get a stereo system
2. **List alternatives**	2. New Used Different features available Quality of sound
3. **State Criteria**	3. Below a certain price Plays both CDs and tapes
4. **Evaluate alternatives**	4. Which meet the criteria? Which has the best sound?
5. **Make a decision**	5. Make a choice Realize what else could have been purchased for the same price (real cost) Decide if the stereo is worth the real cost

Water that licks the hull of this idle riverboat will soon be spilling over its churning paddle wheel, taking tourists and local fun lovers on a Mark Twain-type excursion down the river. Tourism is one of Missouri's primary income resources.

state. The company makes aircraft, missiles, and electronic products at its St. Louis operation. Other big employers in the state include food producers, an airline, a chemical producer, a textile maker, and a package food producer. These are only a few of the many products made in the state.

There can occasionally be economic problems for Missouri, similar to the nation as a whole. With the end of the Cold War, defense cuts have hurt Missouri. Also, with several automobile assembly plants in both St. Louis and Kansas City, downturns in consumer spending can also be hurt. Autos are the second largest purchase, after homes, for buyers and downturns can have immediate effects, such as employee layoffs.

When such downturns occur for a long period, economist say there is a ***recession.*** Unemployment rises when there is a recession and consumer spending declines. Recessions can be severe or moderate and vary in how long they last. If a recession is very severe and lasts a long time, it is called a ***depression.***

The Great Depression of the 1930s led to the "New Deal" and many new government assistance programs. When unemployment is high, there is also greater pressure for government services such as welfare, which were started during the New Deal. Recession means fewer tax revenues coming in at a time when more revenues are needed for governmental assistance programs. Budgets can become unbalanced quickly in this situation.

Economic development has been promoted by state and local governments in an effort to add jobs and increase revenues. The state has been successful in gaining new industry, as have many cities. Expanding existing businesses, though, has been more productive than attracting new ones. More jobs have been created with expansions.

New technology has led to pressures for additional education and employee training. Efforts have been made to upgrade the work force to make them competitive with those in other states. Industry will not build new plants or expand old ones if there are not enough trained employees.

Tourism

Many people come to visit Missouri each year. The tourist industry is created by the spending of these visitors. Tourism is one of the fastest growing parts of the state's economy. It is one of the three most important industries in the state. Tourists spent about five billion dollars in Missouri in 1995. Tourist money supports many kinds of business. These include hotels, restaurants, entertainment, retail trade, and others.

More than one-fourth of the tourists who come here go to the Ozark Mountains. Other major places that tourists visit include Lake of the Ozarks, Kansas City, St. Louis, parks, and historic sites.

The number of tourists coming to Missouri continues to increase. This increases the number of people employed in this industry. The building of more recreational areas should continue to attract more tourists to Missouri. These factors, in turn, help to improve the state's economy.

Agriculture

The third biggest industry in Missouri is agriculture. The different kinds of soil and climate of our state allow many different crops to be grown (soil and climate were discussed in Chapter 1). Three out of four acres of land in the state are used for farming.

Many areas of the state grow specific crops that are best suited to them. This is another example of specialization. Cotton is grown in the southeastern part of the state. Soybeans are grown in many parts of Missouri. Land near the Mississippi and Missouri rivers produces vegetables, grain, and fruit. Corn and wheat are grown in the central and northern areas.

Hay is often grown on the hills where other crops do not do well. The hay crops help to support the large number of dairy and beef cattle. Dairies are centered in the southwestern area. Livestock and animal products make up about half of the agriculture industry in the state. A large number of pigs are also raised in the southwestern area.

Companies that make wood products are major employers in the Ozarks area. They make charcoal, barrel staves, red cedar goods, and produce walnut lumber.

Agriculture is important to Missouri's economy. The state's 108,000 farms produced and sold about $4.82 billion worth of crops, livestock, poultry and aquaculture in 2001, up 3 percent from 2000. Agriculture generally has been so efficient and productive that consumer prices have been kept down. Although farms are small in Missouri, there has been a trend toward larger operations. Competition has increased with factory-type corporate farming, primarily in poultry and pigs. Many families have had to increase the size of their farms to offset the relatively low prices they receive for their products. In addition, more than half of the farmers have taken part-time work away from their farms to subsidize their operations.

Soils in Missouri vary from rich and productive to poor. The Ozark Mountains, for example, have poor soil suitable mostly for grazing and raising timber. In contrast, bottom lands along the major rivers are very rich. A few family farms of sufficient size with rich bottom land are able to be self-sufficient. The rest have problems, but there is such a strong commitment to farming as a way of life that many people are willing to work away from their farms to subsidize their operations. They feel that farming is healthier and provides more freedom than working in the city.

Q:

What are the most important industries in Missouri?

What are the most important things that describe each of the major industries in Missouri?

GOVERNMENT AND THE STATE ECONOMY

Missouri is generally a conservative state. This means Missourians do not generally support big government with its high taxes and many services. The General Assembly has seldom pushed liberal social or economic programs, but the state has adopted some innovative changes. People tend to emphasize individualism and small government. However, there is support for state government to help business where possible, and regulation is tolerated when deemed absolutely necessary.

There is a variety of ways that state government helps business and industry. Incentives have been offered to businesses willing to locate in areas of high unemployment. Cities are authorized by state government to help finance economic development in many ways. Also, many products are excluded from state and local sales taxes to help various industries, for example, paper products used by McDonalds restaurants.

The General Assembly has been supportive of economic development programs for both state and local governments. If economic development is successful, tax revenues can be increased without new taxes; growth adds jobs, and more people working means more tax revenues to the state.

Both state and local governments actively recruit businesses to locate in Missouri. Counties and cities compete for economic growth, as well.

The state treasurer also helps local economies through deposit agreements with special lending institutions that pass on the interest savings to borrowers. This provides low interest loans for jobs, farms, small businesses, water suppliers, housing, and students throughout Missouri.

Q:

Why are the actions of the state government important to the state's economy?

DISCUSSION: WHAT SHOULD THE STATE GOVERNMENT DO ABOUT THE PROBLEMS OF THE UNEMPLOYED AND FARMERS? WHAT OTHER ACTIONS COULD BE TAKEN? SHOULD THE GOVERNMENT BE INVOLVED IN THE ECONOMY?

Heavy machinery eases the final harvest of the season, a bumper crop of soybeans.

SUMMARY

The Missouri economy is based on the goods and services produced in the state. Goods and services are produced by combining the factors of production. Technology and specialization have increased the productivity of workers.

Missouri has a very stable population. There are more than five million people who live in the state. This number is very slowly increasing. Sixty-one percent of these are working age. The people work at many different kinds of jobs. About equal numbers work in manufacturing, trade, and the professions. Still others are farmers or work for the government. People in Missouri have an average income of a little less than the nation as a whole.

Manufacturing is one of the largest industry in the state. A large number of different products are made in Missouri. They are sold around the nation and the world. Tourism is another major industry in the state. Tourists spend money with businesses like hotels, restaurants, and retail stores. Agriculture is a third big industry. The soil and climate allow many different crops to be grown in Missouri. Raising livestock is also a part of the agriculture industry in the state. Some areas of the state specialize in growing certain crops because of their compatibility with the soil and climate.

A healthy economy is needed to provide jobs and a good standard of living for Missouri's people. State government is greatly affected by the economy. If there is a recession, with decreased employment and lowered production, there are fewer tax revenues available for state government. In turn, state government can affect the economy with policies supportive of industry and growth. In addition, it can support education, which is important because businesses need a well trained and educated labor force. Additional revenues have been made available to both lower and higher education over the last decade, as well as new scholarship and loan monies for students.

REVIEW

1. What are the two parts of the economy of a state?
2. What are the factors of production? An example of each.
3. What are the major ways people are employed in Missouri?
4. How does a recession affect different groups of people in Missouri?
5. What kinds of industry are important in Missouri?
6. What are some of the problems of agriculture in Missouri?
7. Why does the state government try to attract new industries to Missouri?
8. Which kind of industry provides more jobs in Missouri than any other industry?
9. Why is the economy important to the state government?
10. Write a brief definition of each of the terms listed under "Terms To Look For" at the beginning of the chapter.

INVESTIGATE

Facts and Figures File:

- Make a list of the different industries that are important to the area of Missouri where you live. Include the products they produce, what kinds of jobs are created by them, the names of the major companies in each industry, and how each of them affects your community.
- The population of Missouri has shown a gradual increase in recent years. This is expected to continue. Find out why the population does not grow as much as some other states in the west and the south.

PROJECT

Choose an industry in the state, such as agriculture or manufacturing. Find out as much as you can about that industry:

- Why is it important to the state?
- How many people are employed by it? What kinds of jobs does it provide?
- In what places in the state is it most important?
- Is it affected by the national economy? How or why not?
- Has it been doing well or poorly recently? Why has this been true?
- What technology does it use?

Add any other information you can find. Interview people who work in this industry, such as a manager, a person who helps with the hiring, and two or three workers. Talk to them about what is happening in their industry today. How is it changing? Put all of this information together into an essay. Remember to start your essay by introducing the topic.

Organize the information in a format that the reader will understand. The conclusion could be what you think will happen to the industry in the future. It could be about the importance of the industry to the state. Just be sure that you can support your conclusion with the information that you have presented.

POINT/COUNTERPOINT

Some people believe that the state government should be active in trying to improve the economy of the state. This would include giving tax breaks to new industries, supporting new small businesses, helping the farmers who are in debt, providing more welfare to the poor, and many other actions.

Others believe that government should stay out of the economy. They do not want to see tax money used to manipulate any segment of the economy.

Read articles about what government should do about the economy in newspapers and magazines. Talk to people who believe in each of these positions. Then choose a position. Write an essay on what you believe and why you believe it. Read your paper to the class and invite the class to ask questions. Be ready to defend your point of view.

❐ SUMMARY OF THE MISSOURI CONSTITUTION

PREAMBLE

"We, the people of Missouri, with profound reverence for the Supreme Ruler of the Universe, and grateful for His goodness, do establish this Constitution for the better government of the State."

Bill of Rights

Article 1 of the Missouri constitution states the basic rights that are guaranteed to citizens, the duties of a citizen, and the principles of government. The following are included as basic rights: freedom of religion, freedom of speech, rights of peaceable assembly and petition, due process of law, trial by jury, right to bear arms, free and open elections, the right to organize and bargain collectively, the right to counsel, to face your accuser, and to a speedy, public trial.

The Bill of Rights states that there will be no unreasonable search and seizure, no suspension of the writ of habeas corpus, no ex post facto laws, no imprisonment for debt, and that no person is required to testify against himself or to be tried for the same crime twice.

Principles of government are also guaranteed by the Bill of Rights. These are some of them: the military is always in subordination to the civil power, citizens are entitled to just compensation for private property taken under the power of eminent domain, and indictments will be determined by grand juries.

The State of Missouri exists as a free and independent state, subject only to the Constitution of the United States. Political power is vested in and derived from the people. State government is intended to promote the general welfare of the people and to guarantee life, liberty, and the pursuit of happiness. The people of the state have the right to regulate the governments and to change the constitution when they think it is necessary.

Separation of Powers

The government of Missouri is divided into three departments: legislative, executive, and judicial. Each department has its own powers and does not conflict with the other departments except when it is permitted by the Constitution.

Legislative Department

The main body of the legislative branch is the General Assembly. It contains the Senate and the House of Representatives. The Senate consists of thirty-four members and the House consists of one hundred and sixty-three members. Senators are elected for four year terms and representatives are elected for two year terms. The qualifications for a senator are: 30 years old, qualified voter for three years, and a resident of the district for one year. The qualifications for a representative are: 24 years old, qualified voter for two years, and a resident of his/her district for one year. No person employed by the United States government, Missouri state government, or a municipality can be elected to the General Assembly. Members of the General Assembly are paid a salary; they also receive a mileage allowance and an expense account as provided for by the law. They are exempt from arrest, except for treason or committing a felony, during the general session and for 15 days before and after the session.

The General Assembly meets on the first Wednesday after the first Monday in January. Bills, however, may be introduced as early as December 1, preceding the session. The General Assembly adjourns at midnight on May 30. Special sessions may be called by the governor or by three-fourths of the members of both houses.

The General Assembly has the power to authorize regulations in regard to a state lottery, the playing of bingo, pari-mutuel betting on horse racing, controlling water pollution, improving drinking water systems, and improving state buildings and property. Through the use of the initiative and referendum, the people retain the right to propose, enact, or reject laws and amendments to the constitution.

Executive Department

The governor has the main responsibility for administering the laws of the state. The qualifications for governor are: 30 years old, citizen of the United States for 15 years and resident of Missouri for 10 years. The governor has the power to appoint people to public office; command the state militia; grant reprieves, commutations and pardons for people convicted of state offenses; and provide information and recommendations to the General Assembly.

Other key officers of the executive department and their duties are:

Lieutenant Governor - ex-officio president of the Senate.

Secretary of State - custodian of all state records and the seal of the state.

State Treasurer - collects taxes and invests the state's monies.

State Auditor - establishes accounting systems for all state officials and agencies.

Attorney General - represents the state in all legal matters.

The order of succession, in case the governor dies, resigns or is impeached, is the lieutenant governor, the president pro tempore of the senate, the speaker of the house, the secretary of state, state auditor, the state treasurer, then the attorney general. No person can be elected governor or treasurer more than twice.

The heads of all the executive departments are appointed by the governor with the consent of the senate. All appointed officers may be removed by the governor. Executive departments include the office of administration, department of agriculture, department of conservation, department of natural resources, department of elementary and secondary education, department of higher education, department of highways and transportation, department of labor and industrial relations, department of public safety, department of revenue, department of social services, and department of mental health.

The governor is required to submit a budget to the General Assembly within 30 days after it convenes. The governor has the power of item veto on any appropriation bill.

Judicial Department

There are three main divisions of courts: the Supreme Court, Court of Appeals and Circuit Courts. The highest court in the state is the Supreme Court. It is composed of seven judges who are appointed by the governor and who hold their sessions in Jefferson City. This court has exclusive appellate jurisdiction over appellate cases involving the Missouri constitution, revenue laws, the title to any state office, criminal cases involving the death penalty, and the statutes of the United States. All other Appelate cases may be handled by the Court of Appeals. The chief justice is selected from one of the seven judges and presides for a term which is determined by the court. Judges are selected for 12-year terms.

The Court of Appeals is organized into districts. There can be no fewer than three districts. Each district has three judges. Judges are selected by the governor for 12-year terms.

The Circuit Courts have original jurisdiction over all civil and criminal cases. Counties are organized together to form a circuit. Each circuit has at least one judge. Judges are selected for 6-year terms.

All judges in the state of Missouri have to be licensed to practice law in the state. Supreme Court judges and Court of Appeals judges must be at least 30 years old, citizens of the United States for 15 years and qualified voters of Missouri for 9 years. Circuit Court judges must be 30 years old, citizens of the United States for 10 years and qualified voters of Missouri for three years.

The courts have the power of judicial review. This allows the courts to examine the legality of rules and orders made by an officer or agency authorized by the state constitution.

Missouri has a non-partisan selection plan for replacing judges. When a vacancy occurs in the Supreme Court, Appeals Court, or Circuit Court, a non-partisan judicial commission submits three names of qualified individuals to the governor who then has 60 days to appoint the nominee. Prior to the end of a term, a judge may declare his or her candidacy for retention by filing a form with the secretary of state. The judge's name then appears on a ballot and voters can either retain or reject the individual.

Judges are prohibited from holding any office in a political party or from taking part in a political campaign. All judges, except municipal judges, are required to retire at age 70.

Local Government

Existing counties in the state are recognized as legal subdivisions. Two or more counties may be joined together through an election. A majority of voters in both counties must approve the consolidation. An election of this type can take place only once in a five year period. A county may be dissolved if two-thirds of the voters approve. Each county seat establishes one town as the county seat. The county seat cannot be moved except by a two-thirds majority of the voters.

If a county has not adopted a special charter, it is managed by a county commission composed of three members. Their job is to manage all county business and to keep an accurate record of its proceedings. The laws of the state allow four classes of counties. All counties within each class have the same powers and are subject to the same restrictions. The terms of county offices are for 4 years.

If a county has more than 85,000 people based on the U.S. census or at least 80,000 people based on the 1970 U.S. census, it may adopt a charter for its own type of government. The charter provides all the powers and duties of the county and its officers. It states the number of county officers, how they are selected, their terms of office and what their salaries will be.

The charter also provides legislative power to the county. This power enables the county to provide services to other municipalities and areas that are not incorporated. However, school districts do not fall under this power. Services that the county provides are contracted and agreed to by both the county and the other municipalities. The county is allowed to impose its own taxes as authorized by the constitution or laws.

To adopt a charter, a county must submit a petition signed by 20 percent of the voters in the last governor's race. The petition is submitted to the county court. Within 60 days, the judge must appoint a commission composed of fourteen freeholders to write the charter. The freeholders are divided equally between the two major political parties and serve without pay. After the charter is written, it must be voted on and approved by a majority of the voters. Notice of the election must be published in at least two local newspapers. If a charter is defeated, it cannot be resubmitted to voters for at least two years.

The General Assembly has also made laws that provide for the organization and classification of cities and towns. There can be no more than four classifications of cities and towns. Each city or town in a particular classification has the same powers and is subject to the same restrictions. Any city or town may contract with another municipality, a political subdivision of another state, or the United States government for the planning, construction and operation of a public improvement or facility.

A city having more than 5,000 inhabitants may also adopt a charter for its own government. The legislative body of the city must submit this question to voters: "Shall a commission be chosen to frame a charter?" Another way a charter can be adopted is by filing a petition signed by 20 percent of the qualified voters. The election then must take place 60 to 90 days after the petition is filed. Candidates for the charter commission are placed on the same ballot and without party designations. The thirteen candidates who receive the highest number of votes become the commission. After the charter is written, it is submitted to the voters for approval. This election must also be publicized in the local newspaper. Amendments to city charters must be approved by a majority of the voters. Amendments may be proposed to the voters by petition, by the legislative body, or by a commission.

Any city or county operating under a charter may pass laws for the clearance and redevelopment of blighted or unsanitary areas. These lands may be used for recreational or other facilities. The land may be taken by the power of eminent domain.

Cities and counties cannot own or lend credit to any form of corporation. A city, by approval of two-thirds of the voters, may construct, improve, or purchase industrial plants. Cities and counties may own their local utilities. They are required to have an annual budget, file annual reports and be audited. A county, city, or school district cannot go into debt without approval of its voters. These same political organizations can approve a debt by popular vote. The vote required is a four-sevenths majority at primary or general elections and a two-thirds majority at all other elections. Cities and counties are also able to issue revenue bonds by a majority vote for the purpose of industrial development, constructing public utility plants, and operating airports.

The City and County of St. Louis

The city of St. Louis is recognized both as a city and a county. It has a city charter to govern its operations. This charter may be amended by a three-fifths majority of the voters. A new or revised charter may be written by a group of thirteen freeholders when authorized by the city lawmaking body. The new or revised charter must also be submitted to the voters. A copy of the new charter must be recorded with the secretary of state and also with the Recorder of Deeds in the city.

The people of St. Louis City and St. Louis County have the power to establish metropolitan districts for common services such as sewers and cultural institutions, to consolidate territory and governments, and to adjust the government as stated by the constitution.

Public Officials

All elected officials of the executive branch of the state and judges of the Supreme Court, Court of Appeals, and Circuit Court may be impeached for the following crimes: misconduct, drunkenness, neglect of duty, incompetency, corruption in office, or moral offenses. The House of Representatives has the sole power of impeachment. All impeachment trials are tried before the Supreme Court except when the defendant is the governor or is a Supreme Court justice. These cases are tried before a special commission of seven well-qualified jurists elected by the Senate. It takes a five-sevenths vote to impeach a person. A person who is impeached may be removed from office. This person may also be tried in a criminal court on the same matter. All officials not subject to impeachment may be removed from office as provided by the law.

If there is a contested election for governor or any other office of the executive branch, the case is heard by the Supreme Court. Other state officials who contest an election will have their cases heard in a lower court of law.

State Employees are prohibited from employing or appointing relatives to state offices.

All state office holders must be citizens of the United States and reside in the state for one year. This requirement may be waived if a person with specialized knowledge or skills is needed in an administrative position. No person may be disqualified from holding office because of sex. All office holders, both civil and military, take an oath of office pledging to support the Constitution of the United States and that of Missouri. The salary earned by state, county and city officials cannot be increased during their term of office nor can their term of office be extended.

Voting and Elections

The general election is held on Tuesday after the first Monday in November of each even-numbered year. This can be changed only when two-thirds of both houses pass a new law.

People may vote in an election if they are citizens of the United States, are 18 years old, have lived in the political subdivision for 30 days and are registered to vote. People may not vote if they are mentally incapacitated, in a mental institution, or are convicted of a felony or a voting crime.

All elections are conducted by secret ballot. Elections may be by written ballot or by any mechanical method approved by law. All elections officers are sworn not to disclose how any voter voted. However, if there is a contested election, a judge may order election officials to testify and the ballots may be opened, examined, and counted as evidence.

Voters may not be arrested while going to, voting, and returning from the polling place except in cases of treason, felony, or violation of the peace. The law provides for absentee voting when a voter cannot attend the election. People who are in the military, attending school, or engaged in civil activities away from their home states are still considered to be residents of their state and may vote by absentee ballot.

Education

The General Assembly is responsible for establishing and maintaining free public schools for all people though age 21. The subdivision of instruction in the public schools is assigned to an eight-member State Board of Education. These are lay people. At no time can more than four members be from the same political party. The term of office is eight years. The Board of Education selects a commissioner of education. The board states the commissioner's duties and compensation. The commissioner then appoints the staff and determines their compensation.

Monies appropriated by the state for public schools is paid at least once a year and distributed according to law. If there is not enough money to keep schools open for 8 months, the General Assembly may provide funds to make up the deficiency. Monies in the public school fund are viewed as being sacredly preserved for education and must be securely invested. No public money is to be used for religious purposes or religious institutions.

The state promotes the establishment and development of free public libraries. Aid is provided to any municipality that supports a free library.

Taxation

The power to tax is given to the General Assembly in order to raise money for the state. The general assembly, in turn, allows counties, cities, and other political subdivisions to levy taxes, including local sales taxes. All taxable property is classified as (1) real property, (2) tangible personal property, and (3) intangible personal property. Taxes can be levied on franchises, incomes, excises, and motor vehicles. All railroad corporations in the state are subject to taxes.

All property, real and personal, of political subdivisions, schools and colleges, religious organizations, charitable organizations, and non-profit agencies are exempt from taxation.

The General Assembly may provide partial relief from taxation on blighted areas or forest areas. The General Assembly has also established a commission to be appointed by the governor with the consent of the senate to equalize assessments between counties.

If the assessed valuation of property increases by a larger percentage than the price level from the previous year, a rollback may be required.

Corporation

The constitution recognizes as corporations all joint stock companies or associations having powers or privileges not possessed by individuals or partnerships. Corporations are organized under the general laws of the state. They are subject to the power and right of eminent domain. Each shareholder in a corporation has the right to cast as many votes as he has shares.

All railways in the state are defined as public highways and railroads as common carriers. Laws are passed to prevent discrimination and extortion on freight rates and passenger rates.

No state bank can be created nor can the state own stock in any corporation or association for banking purposes.

Public Employees

The General Assembly may provide health insurance benefits for state employees and their employees' dependents. Counties, cities, and other political subdivisions may also provide health insurance to their employees and their employees' dependents.

Amending the Constitution

Amendments to the constitution may be proposed at any time by a majority of each house of the General Assembly. All amendments proposed by the General Assembly or by an initiative must be submitted to the voters. The ballot is a separate one and without party designation. The vote may be at a general election or at a special election called by the governor. The proposed amendment should not contain more than one amended or revised article or one new article and should be on the same subject. Information about the proposed amendment should be printed in newspapers in the county, if possible. The amendment is approved by a majority vote and takes effect 30 days after the election.

At the general election in November, 1962, and every 20 years thereafter, the secretary of state is required to submit to the voters the question, "Shall there be a convention to revise and amend the Constitution?" The question is submitted on a separate ballot and without political party designation. If the voters approve, the governor calls for an election of delegates. Fifteen delegates at large and two delegates from each senatorial district are elected. Each delegate must have the same qualifications as a state senator.

The elected delegates must meet within six months of the election. The facilities of the General Assembly are made available for the convention. All delegates must take an oath of affirmation to the Constitution. They receive the same daily rate and mileage as members of the General Assembly. The convention is held in open session. Any changes in the constitution proposed by the convention must be submitted to the voters not less than 60 days nor more than 6 months after the convention. If the changes are approved by the voters, they take effect 30 days after the election.

Because the meanings of new words and concepts in *MISSOURI Studies* are written into the text as they are introduced, this book does not have a glossary. This index will direct you to the page in the textbook where the word or idea is introduced and explained.

Photo Credits:

Jim Bimes: 81, 106; Boone County Sheriff's Office: 81; Columbia Daily Tribune: 95; University of Missouri Extension: 12, 103, 104, 106, 108; Florissant City Police Department, 81; Hardy, Rick-Hardy for Congress campaign photo: 90; Higdon, Bill: 50, 59, 73, 81; Missouri Division of Tourism: 8, 11, 13, 19, 67, 74; Missouri Historical Society: 9, 10; Missouri State Highway Patrol: 46; Missouri House photo by Barbara A. Cochran: 41; Office of the Missouri Secretary of State: 33, 47, 63; Missouri State Senator's offices: 29, 31; Supreme Court of Missouri: 58; Walker-Missouri Tourism: 67; R.W. Wood, Ph.D., University of Missouri Department of Anthropology: 7.